HAD YOU BEEN BORN IN
ANOTHER FAITH

Books by Marcus Bach

THEY HAVE FOUND A FAITH

REPORT TO PROTESTANTS

FAITH AND MY FRIENDS

STRANGE ALTARS

THE WILL TO BELIEVE

THE CIRCLE OF FAITH

GOD AND THE SOVIETS

MAJOR RELIGIONS OF THE WORLD

ADVENTURES IN FAITH

STRANGE SECTS AND CURIOUS CULTS

Fiction

THE DREAM GATE

Had You Been Born in

Prentice-Hall, Inc., Englewood Cliffs, N.J.

MARCUS BACH

Another Faith

The story of religion as it is Lived and Loved
by those who follow the path of their parental faith

Illustrated by Polly Bolian

10 9 8 7 6 5 4 3 2 1

Copyright under International and Pan-American
Copyright Conventions

Library of Congress Catalog Card Number: 61-12979

Printed in the United States of America

ISBN 0-13-372060-8

I feel that the great religions should be viewed as different dialects by which man speaks to God—and God to man.
MARCUS BACH

CONTENTS

To Stand Where Others Stand xiii

1. Had You Been Born a Hindu 1

2. Had You Been Born a Parsi 21

3. Had You Been Born a Buddhist 41

4. Had You Been Born a Confucianist 63

5. Had You Been Born a Shintoist 85

6. Had You Been Born a Jew 103

7. Had You Been Born a Moslem 121

8. Had You Been Born a Roman Catholic .. 147

9. Had You Been Born a Protestant 167

And so it Seems to Me 183

Introduction

TO STAND
WHERE OTHERS STAND . . .

I remember, almost to the hour, when this book was conceived. It was ten years ago on a spring morning, just before
sunrise in Chichicastenango. I had arrived in this enchanted
Guatemalan town late on a Wednesday night, but wakened
early the next morning, for Thursday is market day when
the little village springs to life. This is when the wiry, bare-
footed *cargadores* trudge in from the hills bearing crushing
burdens on their bony backs, when the patient women vendors set out their various wares—ceramics, vegetables, grains
—and when the peasant people from the hills and the valleys, each colorfully dressed in the costume of his clan, trans-
form the ghost city of Chichi into a thriving metropolis.

Curiosity about the religious practices of these people, the
Maya-Quichés, brought me before dawn to the market square.
Here in the mystic light between night and day, I watched
the Mayan priests, short, lithe men in black knee pants, em-
broidered jackets, and red tasseled headgear, fan the sacrificial fires on the pyramid-like steps of aging Santo Tomás
church. As the charcoal mist rose from the braziers, the
priests, swinging their censers, chanting to whatever gods
they knew, moved back and forth and up and down the

steps in a setting as mysterious as something out of the legends of Montezuma.

The church, although once Roman Catholic, had reverted to the primitive practices of the people it had tried in vain to convert. In fact, the Catholic clergy had moved out and the animistic Mayans, in a pageantry of incense, smoke, and the incessant beating of muffled drums, were re-instating their own immortal deities.

As I watched, the Maya-Quiché worshipers climbed the steps, pausing to buy a candle from a vendor, which the Mayan priests blessed with a swish of the censer. Then the worshiper bowed and passed through the huge black doors.

Drawn by the mystery of worship, I, too, bought a candle and climbed the steps through the blue smoke curling against the church's whitewashed walls. As a colorful, bare-legged Mayan cleric, with a red cap placed almost jauntily on his head, waved the smoking censer in front of me, he said something I could not understand, but when he graciously bowed as if to say I should enter, I followed the worshipers inside.

Now I was behind the massive doors. In a spacious, vaulted sanctum without pews, where a few statues of Christian saints gazed down in wonder from their niches in the walls and where a votive light still burned, the natives sat on the floor amidst pools of burning candles. It was a garden of flickering lights. Huddled figures crouched guardedly over their tapers. There a mother nursed her child and here a father guided his small son's hand as he lit his white ritual candle.

It struck me then that these people, most of whom had nothing in the world save a mountain shack on a plot of rocky ground, or a herd of goats, or yarn to weave, or clay for fashioning pottery, were now suddenly rich in life and spirit. They had passed through the mist and the forbidding doors and were now, by way of incantations and the offerings of their faith, identified with something beyond themselves. The hopeless disorder around me took on a semblance of order. The tallow-spattered floor and the disarray were part of the ritual. Watching these devotees and hearing their murmured, *"Ahau Ah Tohil. . . . Ahau Ah Gucumata. . . ."* I sensed that they devoutly believed their God or gods were good.

I knelt beside an old man and, by means of an inquiring glance, asked him if I might light my candle from his. As he nodded and turned toward me, I could see the secret pride in his eyes and together we watched the flicker of his candle as it lighted mine. Turning away again, he closed his eyes tightly, as if to resume his prayer.

As I fixed my candle to the floor and gazed into its light, something within me said, "What if you had been born in this man's faith?"

And that is when this book was conceived.

The years of gestation were nourished by visits to the temples of other people in other cultures and in other lands. Some little-known. Some well-known. I was admitted to a Parsi's temple in Calcutta where non-Parsis are commonly forbidden. I knelt in the oldest Moslem mosque in Damascus. I visited synagogues in Israel, Shinto shrines in Japan, Buddhist stupas and pagodas in Asia, and walked among Confucian graves in the hills beyond Hong Kong. I meditated in Hindu ashrams in India and at the holy ghats along the sacred Ganges. I stood in the Sikh's Golden Temple at Amritsar, and joined the people in Eastern Catholic cathedrals in the Kremlin and in Roman Catholicism's St. Peter's in Rome. I worshiped in the churches of Europe which memorialized the Reformation. I took part in the meetings in Voodoo *hounforts* and was allowed inside a *morada* of the Penitentes.

It was not only the variety of beliefs that intrigued me. It was, rather, the worshiper himself, and what he found or felt that he had found that aroused my interest and response.

Most of all, I was impressed by my own realization that we understand others best when we understand what they believe, and that we can never truly enter into their belief until we stand for a little while where these people stand.

Of course, this requires a bit of doing. To live, for a little while, in the orbit of the other person's deepest convictions means that we must momentarily leave the spot where years of stubborn indoctrination have rooted us. We must move into the spiritual habitue of another's mind and heart; we must become, for a time at least, one with those whose way of life and type of worship and even whose physical make-up we have viewed, up to now, only through the fixed focus of our own cherished points of view. To change, for one enchanted moment, the bent of our soul, the set of our mind, and, where necessary, even the color of our skin, is quite an assignment.

But since we must learn to live together or none of us will live, what else is there to do? And since we have tried every other known avenue for understanding, why not try this? And inasmuch as we are all mortal immortals, living for a little while in our impermanent world, and then going on to live again, why should we not embark on this greatest of all adventures?

And when we have done this and identified ourselves with the major religions of the world, what happens to us? What happens to our faith, whatever our faith may be?

What do we learn?

What do we find?

Where do we go from here?

It was not only to answer questions of this kind that this book was written, but to answer another question that you, too, perhaps have often asked yourself, "Had I been born in another faith, what would my faith—and I—be like?"

1

Had You Been Born
a Hindu

Had you been born a Hindu, your birthplace would very likely have been somewhere in India. Of the 350,000,000 Hindus in the world, all but 20,000,000 live in the Asian subcontinent. Followers of your religion are found in Ceylon, South Africa, Thailand, and in other parts of the world, but the faith began in India, and India is its promised land.

As a child you would have been surrounded by the sights and sounds of a country steeped in religious tradition. You would have walked through streets which sheltered sacred cows and were friendly to holy men. You would have heard the tantalizing tones of temple bells, and seen the faithful as they brought their offerings of fruit and money to the village shrines.

YOUR HINDU HOME

One of your earliest memories would be that of your family altar: a small, wooden shelf in your parental home. As a child

1

you sat in meditation in front of this holy place while your
mother's *mantras* (prayers) crept tenderly into your life,

"Thou, God, art the cherished guest in our humble home.
Thou art father, brother, son, friend, benefactor, guardian,
all in one. Deliver us, thy worshipers, from the taint of sin
and, O Mighty Lord, when we die, deal mercifully with us
on that final day."

Although your family worshiped at the altar at many stated
times and on many holy days and holy nights, Thursday morning
was always a special day. For it was on this morning that your
mother never took food until she had performed her altar duties.
She put a fresh flower and a bowl of rice on the altar before she
seated herself in prayer. As she knelt there, she seemed to have
entered for a little while into a mysterious world of her own.

Your mother had a streak of vermilion in her hair, and she
once explained to you that years ago at the marriage ceremony,
when she and your father sat before the holy fire, your father
had dipped his finger into the vermilion paste and had made the
mark upon her hair to signify the enduring holiness of marriage.
This sign, which your mother renewed every Thursday morning,
was a rite which held a deep meaning for her.

She also wore a small iron bracelet which had been placed
around her wrist by your father during the wedding ceremony.
Ever after that, whenever she worshiped, she included in her
prayers the words, "O God, give us peace and quietude of heart.
Grant long life to my husband." You were told that only if your
father should die would the bracelet be taken off and broken.

All the articles on the altar were holy: incense to remind you
of the love and fragrance of the gods and of your love for them;
fresh flowers, proof of your adoration; rice and candy, symbols of
your thankfulness for heaven's blessings; a lovely conch representing life, for life began on the floor of the sea; and a small bell, a
sign of invocation and welcome to the gods.

Most important, however, among the altar furnishings was a
statue of Krishna, the eighth avatar of Vishnu, and one of Lakshmi,
the goddess of wealth. These were the gods of your home, but
you were taught that other Hindu altars had other gods, for one

of the great glories of Hinduism is that there are enough gods and goddesses for every class and for every type of person everywhere. *Every Hindu has the liberty to choose the god and the worship which seem best for him and which best express some deep response in his soul.* There are great gods and little gods, just as there are great people and little people, but every god, even as every person, serves a specific purpose in the mysterious web of life.

THE GODS OF HINDUISM

Had you been born a Hindu, you would move familiarly among the vast "families" of gods. You would know that Vishnu, the Preserver, has many avatars or reincarnations of which Krishna is one of the most important. You would understand that Shakti is the goddess of universal energy; Indra, the king of gods and goddesses; Varuna, the all-seeing god of the waters; Agni, the god of fire; Ganesh, the elephant god, symbol of wisdom and prudence and good luck. You would honor Sarasvati, goddess of learning, and be delighted with Hanuman, the monkey god who, according to legend, spanned the watery distance between India and Ceylon in one mighty leap.

You would not be confused by the fact that Shakti is also called Uma and Bhavani and Devi and Parvati and Durga. As a Bengali Hindu you would look forward eagerly to the great autumn festival when Durga is honored in a mighty *puja* or worship-ceremony. Shakti is also Kali, the goddess of storms and disaster, and you would remember the many times your parents took you to pay respect to Kali in her many temples. Temples to the gods and the goddesses stand in every village, in every town, in every city. Altars and shrines are found wherever Hindus are found, for your religion, more than any other, brings gods and men into an inter-related household of faith.

In spite of numerous deities and avatars, you would know that Hinduism actually offers its believers but one God. *God is one though He is many.* He is so many that sometimes you use a string of beads to help you remember God's many names. But with all His names and images, He is one. This was explained to you when your father told you that all humanity is also one, although it has millions of forms and expressions.

When you asked your father, "Who is the one God?" you were told, "He is Brahma." And when you persisted, "Who and what is Brahma?" he said, "Brahma is the World-Soul. Brahma is Cosmic Consciousness, the Atman or Breath of Life, the Absolute, the Principle of Love and Law."

It was explained to you that all religions have difficulty in defining God. You were informed that Christians also have many names for God. They call Him Jehovah, Lord, Father Almighty, God of Gods, King of Kings. Some Christians say that God is Jesus Christ, or God is a Spirit. Others identify Him with Love, Justice, Creative Intelligence, Life, Mercy, Power, Compassion, and many more such attributes.

Had you been born a Hindu, you would also think of your God, Brahma, as having many attributes; yet he would remain the Supreme One, the timeless, limitless essence of the universe. Of course, many Hindus actually worship these *attributes*, just as people in other religions worship such qualities of God as Love, Wisdom, and Service, but this is only because the mind of man cannot fully comprehend the mind of God. Hinduism, however, tries to comprehend Brahma because Hinduism is fully as much a philosophy as it is a religion.

You would remember a day when you walked with your father along the holiest of rivers, the Ganges, and watched the scores of faithful worshipers sitting on the bank of this sacred stream. One of them, a half-starved man, sat cross-legged in front of the statue of Krishna with the flute. How long this old man had been gazing at this image no one could say. Perhaps for months or years. He was in a trance-like state. His body looked as if it were molded out of clay. It seemed to you that he had stopped breathing. Your father said, "He is in a state of *samadhi*, a world of the spirit. He is face to face with the Infinite and perhaps merged into it." People of other religions might have asked what good the man was doing or what he was accomplishing or whether it was really true that he was "face to face with the Infinite." But because you had been born a Hindu, you would have agreed with your father when he explained, "Who knows by looking at the outward appearance of a man what is going on in his heart?"

THE SPELL OF HINDUISM

Your initiation into your faith would have come at the age of thirteen. At that time a Hindu priest and many of your relatives gathered in your home for the traditional "thread ceremony" when, in a solemn and sacred ritual, your head was shaved as you sat with your father in front of the holy fire. After the priest had pierced your ears with a needle, signifying that you were ready to assume your full religious duties, he gave you the sacred thread. You held it in your left hand, palm forward, in front of your face with your right hand behind your head. Your eyes were fixed in meditation upon the thread while the priest chanted a prayer of dedication. For a moment you, too, came "face to face with the Infinite," as you meditated upon the true Self which is God in you. The true Self, you told yourself, *is* God. When your father whispered to you the holiest and most ancient of all mystical words: *Om*, you repeated it with deep reverence. "*Om—Om*," you whispered, and it seemed to you as though a greater life had been added to your life and a deeper breath to your breath.

"*Om* is indeed Brahma," your father said. "*Om* is the highest and greatest reality that man can conceive. Whoever knows *Om* obtains all he desires. *Om* is the best support. Whoever understands *Om* is adored in the world of Brahma."

With the mystical *Om* fixed in your mind and heart, you were taken into a darkened room. When the door closed, the silence and aloneness greatly disturbed you, but gradually they were overcome by the feeling of a Presence. You were left alone in this room for three days with whatever your thoughts of God might be. For three days you remained in the silent dark as motionless as the holy men whom you had seen on the bank of the holy Ganges. In accordance with instructions given you by the priest, you

> Put outward thoughts aside
> And the eyes in the midst of the brows,
> Making the outward and inward breaths
> Equal in their course within the nostrils. . . .

That is how you meditated while the mystical *Om* became ever more meaningful to you in your monastic cell. For three days, as you actually lived the life of a secluded monk, you realized what the monks and the holy men thought, what they felt and what the Presence of God meant to them.

Noises from the out-of-doors broke into your thoughts: the sound of an automobile, the rumble of a bullock cart, the cry of a vendor, the laughter of boys your age. These were the temptations of freedom of which the priest spoke. But if you were to follow them, if you were to give in to desire, you would know no peace. For a moment you might have wished with all your heart that you could escape from this faith-imposed prison, but then you came to realize that the room was not a prison. The walls did not confine you. They shielded you from the world so that you could better find the Self within you which is God. That was the lesson you sought to learn: *God and I are one.* You said it over and over, *"God and I are one."* Being one with Him, you also became one with all people. The *mantras* (prayers) helped you. A lovely thought from the holy book, the Upanishads, came to your mind and you repeated it softly to yourself:

> He who sees himself in all beings,
> And all beings in himself,
> He enters the supreme Brahma
> By this means and no other.

The hours passed. There in the darkness you began to understand what the holy men meant when they said that Brahma is found in the search for Him. More loudly now you said, *"Om—Om—Om,"* and for a little while there was no feeling of loneliness at all. You had unlocked the inner consciousness of faith.

The door to your "cell" opened, sending a flood of light into the room. Blindly you saw the outline of the priest who had come, as promised, to look into your state of mind and soul. Closing the door, he seated himself cross-legged in front of you and for a long time no word was spoken. The street sounds did not tempt you any longer. You felt honored that the priest had come, but you knew too, that honor is close to pride and that pride is close to sin.

You knew that soon your mother would come and place food—rice and a few cold vegetables—before you. You were sure that she was thinking constantly about you during your three days of retreat and that she was concerned about you. But courageously you remembered that true holy men do not think of food; they do not wish to be remembered and they would not be lured in any way from Brahma and His love. While thinking and with the silent priest seated before you in the shadows, you advanced from childhood into the maturity of spiritual understanding.

THE HINDU TRINITY

Your religious development continued. You learned the meaning of a Sanskrit word: *Trimurti*. It means a triad or something grouped in threes. Most of all, it refers to the Hindu trinity: Brahma, the Creator; Vishnu, the Preserver; Shiva, the Destroyer.

You learned, as all Hindus do, that Brahma, the Creator, first person in the trinity, is depicted as a god with four heads. This is an attempt to show that He is all-seeing and all-knowing and that nothing in the world escapes Him. By Him the world was made. Indeed, He made the world in such fashion that it will endure for a cycle of 4,320,000,000 years; then it will be destroyed, but will be re-established for another cycle, and another and another, through time everlasting. Each such cycle of billions of years of creation and destruction is but a day and a night for Brahma.

You were taught that Vishnu, the Preserver, second person of the trinity, sustains the world during each of its many cycles. Pictures of him pass through your mind. He has been depicted as a dwarf, a fish, a lion, a tortoise, as many other animals, and as a man. This is the symbology which interprets him as the all-knowing one. There is no phase of life which Vishnu has not experienced, and so you worship him as omnipresent, for he is in all and over all and all life is holy because of Vishnu.

You came to understand Shiva, the Destroyer, third person in the Trimurti, for when you asked a friend about the origin of evil and suffering in the world, he referred to Shiva.

"Evil," the priest told you, "comes from a source deep within Brahma, and that part of Brahma from which it comes is Shiva. Though Shiva destroys, He also recreates. If He destroys, it is for the purpose of providing an opportunity for renewal, and for an awakening to greater enlightenment. This is regeneration. *Shiva who destroys, also redeems.* This is to say that *the nature within you which seeks to do evil, also seeks to do good. Evil is illusion, but the illusion exists. To believe that it exists is in itself evil.*"

It was wonderful to have a teacher who *knew,* even though you did not fully understand his knowing! Priests and holy men also sought to familiarize you with the meaning behind the myths and legends of your faith. They pointed out that stories and parables were often employed by the early interpreters of Hinduism as a means for transmitting important truths to the people. The masses, unable to understand the deepest significance of the true realities involved in the faith, were, nonetheless able to recognize some personalization within the stories themselves. Legends, your teachers assured you, are vessels holding hidden truths. When you were disturbed by the difficult subject of caste, it was explained by a wise teacher by way of an ancient story.

THE LEGEND OF CASTE

Once upon a time, says the legend, there was a god, Purusa, who told Brahma he would be willing to sacrifice himself so that man might be created. When Brahma agreed to this proposal, Purusa was sacrificed on the altar of heaven where, under Brahma's direction, a mighty miracle took place. Out of Purusa's mouth priests were created, priests called Brahmans. Out of his arms came warriors called Ksatriyas. Out of his thighs sprang business people, the Vaisyas. And from his feet emerged the menial laborers, the Sudras. All of these people were different, but all were also alike in that they all represented parts of Purusa the god.

You meditated on this legend as your teacher pointed out that caste is a word of many meanings. In ancient Sanskrit the word for caste is *varna,* and *varna* means color. The light-skinned Aryans who came down the Indus River considered themselves of a higher caste or color than the darker-skinned Indus (Hindu) inhabitants. Caste also means a difference in intellectual ability, in economic and social standing, in occupation and profession. Some people were so low in the social scale that they were not included in any of the four castes. They were outcastes and untouchables.

Though the importance and rigid separation of caste are changing now, you often ask yourself, "Why did the great God Brahma permit people to be different in ability, in color, and in station in life?" The legend of Purusa does not fully explain why today some people are born rich, others poor. Some are wise and fortunate and healthy and happy, others are not. Some die young and others live to be very old. Why?

Had you been born a Hindu, you would have come to a satisfactory conclusion about these questions. You would have learned that a man is what he is in respect to his caste, his fortune and his place in life because of the "wheel of justice" which Brahma set in motion at the beginning of time, even before the creation of man *and the wheel of justice is known as Karma.*

THE LAW OF KARMA

Karma, you were taught, inexorably fixes the consequences of one's acts. *A person is what he is because of his Karma, which is destiny in action.* Karma cannot be tampered with, altered, influenced or destroyed. It is neither good nor bad. Karma simply *is.* It pertains to lives lived before and to lives which will be lived again, for the lives of gods and men have been lived and relived many times.

Had you been born a Hindu, you would be convinced that there is no other answer to the mystery of life and no clear explanation for the seeming inequality in the world than the answer found in the Karmic law. Karma assures and warns you that nothing you do goes unrewarded. Nothing is ever unaccounted for. Nothing is forgotten, discarded, or of no account. Your character and your station in life are determined by the acts, thoughts, desires, hopes and plans for which you are directly responsible.

Though the law of Karma cannot be changed, it can be influenced through the intercession of the gods. With their help you can overcome evil by doing good. With their help you can build up a good Karma. You can prepare yourself for a better station in the next life by living virtuously in this life. What you are in your present life is the consequence of what you have been; what you may be in your next life depends upon what you do in this one. Slowly, man lifts himself through the repetition of lives to reach an ultimate peak of perfection.

Your teachers explained these concepts to you and made them part of your spiritual orientation. They also told you about Karma's inseparable counterpart: Reincarnation.

THE DOCTRINE OF REINCARNATION

Reincarnation is the cycle of living experiences in which the soul of man—his psyche, *Atman,* or life essence—makes its eternal round of births and rebirths. For if a person is to reap the rewards of his deeds (Karma), it is logical that he must not only live *again,* but that he has also lived *before* in an earlier incarnation.

Karma and Reincarnation provide a solution to the perplexing puzzle of why one person dies young and another one lives to old age. Reincarnation explains the phenomenon of a genius, the reason for prodigies. It sustains you in your conviction that God is just and true; and it reminds you that, if you meet the burdens and challenges of this life valiantly, you will be rewarded when you return for another pilgrimage on this earthly plane. Even more, Reincarnation prepares you for eventual union with Brahma in a state of immortal bliss. For the soul which bore you is the World-Soul. You came from it and to it you will return. "Never have I not been," said Krishna to a student, "never hast thou not been, and never shall the time come when we shall not be."

LIFE IS A CLASSROOM

Had you been born a Hindu, you would look upon life in the

world as a classroom. Death is a final examination. After death you remain in heaven as long as your good Karma allows you to stay, or it may be that you remain in hell as long as your bad Karma holds you there. After you serve your time in heaven or hell, you return to earth to qualify again for the courses in which you previously failed, or to take the advanced work for which a previous life has prepared you.

THE HINDU SCRIPTURES

The Hindu holy books, very old and full of wisdom, help you in your understanding of the cycles of life. Had you been born a Hindu, you would have been taught that these books were conceived by Brahma Himself and transmitted to the world through inspired holy men, the Rishis, who perpetuated them through oral tradition for at least a thousand years before the sacred words were written down.

Among these books are the holy Vedas. Veda means wisdom and spiritual insight, and the more than 100 Vedic books are so important that the years during which they were composed, 1500 to 800 B.C., are known as the Vedic period. Four books are of special importance: the Rig-Veda, which contains 1028 hymns; the Sama-Veda, a book of revelation; the Yajur-Veda, a collection of hymns and prayers; the Artharva-Veda, a series of charms and incantations.

You would have memorized many beautiful passages from these scriptures and learned to chant the stirring hymns, like the one to Surya, god of the sun:

> By lustrous heralds led on high
> The fire-Sun ascends the sky;
> His glory draweth every eye.
>
> The stars which gleamed throughout the night,
> Now slink away like thieves in fright,
> Quenched by the splendor of thy might.

Hymns to the god Varuna would also have become a part of your spiritual treasury:

> He knows the path of birds that through
> The atmosphere do wing their flight,
> And, ocean dwelling, knows the ships.
>
> He knows the pathway of the wind,
> The wide, the high, the mighty wind,
> And those who sit enthroned above.
>
> Enthroned within his palace sits
> The god Varuna whose law is firm,
> All-wise for universal sway.
>
> From there the observant god beholds
> All strange and secret happenings,
> Things that are done or to be done.

You would have learned to chant the prayer of faith:

> Faith in the early morning,
> Faith at noonday will we invoke;
> Faith at the setting of the sun,
> O Faith, endow us with belief!

Another holy book, the Bhagavad-Gita, would hold a prominent place in your life. It is part of the famous Mahabharata—an epic of 220,000 lines, longest in the world—and records a dialogue between the warrior Arjuna and the god Krishna, who is his charioteer. Here in the Gita you find rules for the conduct of the true Hindu. Its pages urge you to live the kind of life out in the world that you lived during the three days of your initiation, "Holding in indifference alike pleasure and pain, gain and loss, conquest and defeat, so make thyself ready for the struggle, thus shalt thou not fall into sin."

In the inspired Gita, Krishna describes the kind of follower he loves: "Desireless, pure, skillful, impartial, free from terrors, who renounces all undertakings and worships me, he is dear to me. He who rejoices not, hates not, grieves not, desires not, who renounces alike fair and foul, and has devotion, is dear to me. One indifferent to foe and friend, indifferent in honour and dishonour, in heat and cold, in joy and pain, free of attachment, who holds in equal account blame and praise . . . silent, content with whatsoever befalls, homeless, firm of judgment, possessed of devotion, is a man dear to me."

To be dear to Krishna, to live the life of tranquillity, wisdom, and faith, these would have been your chief objectives, had you been born a Hindu. That is why you would also turn to the holy books, the Aranyakas, for instructions on how the will and wishes of Brahma may be attained. Here in the Aranyakas, you would find suggestions for:

THE FOUR STAGES OF LIFE

1. The period of student life or discipleship.
2. The period of family life or householder.
3. The period of contemplation or forest-dwelling.
4. The period of total spiritual commitment or asceticism.

Had you been born a Hindu, you would follow these four stages to a greater or lesser degree depending upon your devotion to the faith. Thus, during the early period of your life you would have been a serious student, realizing that no sharp line could be drawn between what is secular and what is spiritual. You would have studied and discussed religion with your parents and teachers. In all probability you would have found your own *guru,* a holy man—like your priest—who would have imparted special advice, and in whose example you would have found a pattern for your words and deeds. You would have loved and respected this *guru* so much that you would have placed his picture above your altar. When you thought about his faith, your faith increased; when you meditated on his life, your own life was enriched. "How else can I learn," you would often have asked, "but through someone who has learned?"

During this period of discipleship you might also have begun the study and practice of yoga. Yoga is a science of spiritual development based upon pure thought, pure actions, pure breathing, pure exercises and pure awareness. You would have sought an accredited yogi as your practitioner who would have helped you acquire control over nature and teach you how to unfold your psychic powers. He would have instructed you how to make the mystical *Om* a usable substance in your physical and mental life. He would have taught you the proper use of food, the secrets of health, and the amazing powers of self-control. Brahma himself says in the holy Gita, "Yoga is the destroyer of misery to him who is well controlled in eating, working and sleeping." Yoga is union with God.

Unless you had decided to become a yogi or join an ashram (spiritual retreat) for the remainder of your life, you would have entered the second stage advised by the Aranyakas, that of a householder. In keeping with tradition, your marriage would have been arranged by your parents. Together with the parents of your bride-to-be, they would have consulted the astrological charts in order to determine whether you were suited to each other and to select the most auspicious time for your marriage.

Your wedding ceremony in front of the holy fire would have been a solemn and sacred event. Here you re-enacted the custom of placing the vermilion on the forehead of your bride and clasping the iron bracelet around her wrist. You were asked to keep sacred a Hindu axiom, "Marriage should be the beginning, not the end of romance." And, as often happens, you would not have seen the person you were to marry until shortly before the ceremony. This would matter little if you had been born a Hindu, for you would trust the judgment of your parents and the guidance of the gods in the selection of your mate. Giving your hand in marriage, you would have said, "I take hold of your hand for good fortune so that, with you, we may attain old age. I am the words and you are the melody; I am the melody and you are the words."

After you had established your home and your children were grown, you might have entered the third phase: the life of a "forest-dweller." Devoting yourself to philosophical study, which the hard work of making a living for your family had deprived you, you would take a renewed interest in religion. With maturity of thought you would seek to further deepen your knowledge of Hinduism.

Perhaps you would have followed Vedanta, one of the most modern and popular schools of thought whose foremost interpreter,

Shankara, lived in the eighth century. It was Shankara who said: "Brahma is the only reality. All else, the world and life, are *maya* or illusion." Shankara explained how *moksha* or salvation is attained by the realization that we are all caught in veils of illusion of which we can rid ourselves only through wisdom, the wisdom that Brahma is the World-Soul and that our soul is, in truth, the soul of Brahma. *"I am that I am . . . yonder Person (God) I am He,"* are the profoundest truths, and Shankara would have been your helper in their understanding.

Or you might have plunged into Vaisheshika metaphysics during your "forest-dwelling" period, or interested yourself in the Nyaya school of logic, or in Purva Mimansa, which insists that the Universe is real, that happiness is a legitimate goal, and that Dharma (religion, righteousness) is the pathway to spiritual peace. As if preparing for the "final examination," you would hold in your heart the knowledge that your earthly sojourn must have an end; therefore, you would dwell in the forest of ideas thoughtfully and with a deepened reverence for life.

Then, according to the Aranyakas, you would be ready to consider the final stage, that of the wandering ascetic. You would contemplate seriously on the idea of renouncing your family, possessions and self to begin a lonely life of wandering with begging bowl and staff in the role of a *sannyasin,* an especially dedicated holy man.

Had you been born a Hindu, the challenge of complete renunciation would be laid upon your heart by the dictates of your religious culture. At the age of sixty or sixty-five—or earlier—you would take the counsel of the Aranyakas seriously and say, "I will give up my work and my estate and devote the remainder of my life to spiritual asceticism. My wife will enter a Hindu convent and I will become a *sannyasin.* Our family is grown. We have tasted the world. It is now time for us to give the remaining years to God in a special way."

You could not escape the challenge. The holy men of India, past and present, speak to you. The spirit of the holy books calls out to you. Even the holy cows and the festivals with their music and incense, the sound of the gongs, the sight of men praying in the streets, all seem to ask, "How do you stand with Brahma now that life is waning and another life is dawning?"

THE CHALLENGE OF THE SANNYASIN

Something says to you, "Become a *sannyasin*. He walks alone in the lonely places. He chants his prayers after other worshipers have left the temple squares. He kneels at the shrines and washes in the Holy Ganges and wherever he goes he carries with him a serenity and an inner light which you, with all your achievements, do not have."

The *sadhus* (holy teachers) would lay the burden of the *sannyasin* upon you, saying, "When you live in society, you judge yourself by the standards of society. When you live with monks or contemplatives, you judge yourself by the standards of their lives. It is only when you live and wander alone as a *sannyasin* that you have no other standard but God by which to measure your virtue."

The words would express your point of view, had you been born a Hindu. Whether or not you took them literally, they would echo in your heart and mind, tantalizing you to close your earthly life in the role of a holy pilgrim. Wisdom has always come by way of the four stages which the Aranyakas have set forth in clear, beguiling terms.

Because of the *sannyasins* in Hinduism, you would admire and respect the holy men of *all* religions and *all* countries. You see in all prophets the full expression of your unfinished greatness. Often you feel like saying with the eminent *sadhu*, T. L. Vaswani, "When alone and in the depth of silence, I have, methinks, seen the face of Jesus in the village folk, on the faces of the wanderers, and in the countenances of little children. I have communed with Him in the cottages of the poor. I have seen Him among the sick. In little acts of kindness, in seemingly unspiritual things, I have received His benediction. He is a rare spirit in history. His life was love and His crown was meekness."

Had you been born a Hindu, you would insist that Hinduism is interested in every man who has made God more real to a quest-

ing world. For your faith is non-sectarian. It knows no denominational lines. It sends out no missionaries. It believes "all roads that
lead to God are good." It strives to meet the quest of every seeker
no matter what his caste or the outreach of his mind may be.

HINDUISM IS MANY THINGS

Hinduism is many things to you. It is the influence of a Gandhi
who, renouncing worldly goods and proclaiming that his people
could not rightly serve God while "enslaved," instigated a movement which eventually set India free. You revere Gandhi very
much and you often pause before his statues which are seen in
many public squares. You visit his shrine at Gandhighat in Delhi
where, in keeping with Hindu custom, his body was cremated.
You feel the presence of his divine nature and remember that just
before he died he asked forgiveness for his assassin. All of this is
in the spirit of your faith.

Hinduism is also the work of Vinoba Bhave, one of Gandhi's
disciples, who for many years has walked from village to village,
persuading rich landowners to divide their land with the poor
and the refugees. "What the world desperately needs," says
Bhave, "is changed lives, lives that will demonstrate stewardship
and honor God through sharing."

Hinduism is the activity of the Ramakrishna monks, a society
of dedicated men inspired by the *sannyasin*, Ramakrishna, and
his disciple, Vivekananda. They have developed orphanages and
schools, hospitals and rehabilitation centers throughout India and
in many parts of the world.

Hinduism is the accomplishment of Dr. M. Modi, India's
famous eye specialist. A quiet-spoken, mild-mannered Hindu,
trained in American and European medical schools, he is a living
example of selfless service. He travels from village to village,
working unceasingly in "eye camps" to help the millions of blind
and near-blind in the sub-continent. You hear him say, "The
people are my god. The operating room is my temple. The instruments are my *puga* (worship)."

To you, Hinduism is many things: it is the philosophy of the
eminent scholar, Dr. Sarvepalli Radhakrishnan; the wisdom of

the remarkable leader, Jewaharlal Nehru; the poetry of Rabindranath Tagore; the profound and practical thought of Sri Aurobindo. It is the work of Ram Mahun Ray, who founded the Brahmo Samaj (Fellowship of God) and was instrumental in abolishing the custom of *sati*, (the burning of the widow on the funeral pyre of departed husband). It is the work of translators in India's universities and the inspiration of India's thousands of holy men. Hinduism is all this and most of all, it is the hope of those who, no matter what their class or caste, feel within themselves the call of Brahma. And hearing his call, they say with the Gita, "My bewilderment has vanished. I have gotten remembrance by thy grace. I stand freed from doubt. I will do thy word."

AND SO TO DIE—AND THEN TO LIVE AGAIN

The word of faith is life. There is no death for you, had you been born a Hindu. True, at the time of transition, your body will be burned and your ashes scattered into a holy river. As a Hindu, you would have often watched the colorfully shrouded corpses being lifted to the funeral pyres along the banks of the Mother Ganges and have waited while the fire consumed the body. Had you been born a Hindu, you would have lighted your father's funeral pyre, just as your son will one day light the sandalwood upon which your body will be placed. You would have heard the incantations and the hollow sound of the conch shells as they were blown, the ecstatic wail of the hymns and the strains of the plaintive instruments while *Om, Om* rang in your heart and mind. But deep in your soul you would have been assured that though sadness and weeping mingled with the funeral flames, there is no death.

Death is merely a release and a beginning again. You would find comfort in the thought that when the time comes for your release, you will remember the admonition of the Vedas, "Let your eye go to the Sun and your life to the Wind. By the meritorious acts that you have done, go to heaven and then come to the earth again; or resort to the waters if you feel at home there; or remain in the herbs with the bodies you propose to take."

Had you been born a Hindu, you would know what these

words imply. Silently you would watch as the flames carry some beloved soul to heaven; thoughtfully you would sense the presence of God; confidently you would tell yourself that all life is a cycle, all is Karma and Reincarnation.

True, Hinduism is in transition. India is in transition. So are all religions and all lands. Old temples fall into decay, old customs become outmoded, old beliefs are often neglected and left to die. New eras, industrialization, new thoughts, a shrinking world cause your religion to tremble beneath the giant hand of change. But always there has been, always there is, and always there will be the one and eternal Brahma, changeless and eternal.

Perhaps somewhere along the way of your Hindu experience you heard of a western philosopher, Emerson, who so loved and respected your faith that he caught the spirit of all that you believe and immortalized it in his *Brahma* when he wrote the meaningful words:

> "If the red slayer thinks he slays,
> And if the slain thinks he is slain,
> He knoweth not my subtle ways,
> I turn and pass and turn again. . . ."

These lines would be understood by no one better than by you, had you been born a Hindu.

2

Had You Been Born
a Parsi

HAD YOU BEEN BORN A PARSI, you would often kneel before a fire burning in a large brass urn in the temple of your faith. The vaulted room is fragrant with the scent of sandalwood and as the white-robed priest lays another polished stick on the flames, you whisper a prayer as other members of your religion have done through countless centuries. In some Parsi temples the fire, fed by the hands of the faithful, has been burning uninterruptedly for more than a thousand years.

You would know that the source of the original fire was a lightning flash. This was the elemental flame sent to earth by Ahura-Mazda, the supreme deity and guardian of mankind. Somewhere in a forest when this lightning struck, one of your ancestors captured some of the sparks or flames and from these were kindled all other fires in the temples of your religion. Fire is a sacred symbol of your faith.

PARSIISM, AN ANCIENT AND VENERABLE RELIGION

Your religion is one of the oldest and one of the smallest, numerically, in the world. It has had few, if any, converts. A person must be born into it and that is why it numbers only slightly more than 100,000 followers, almost all of whom live in India and most of them in and around Bombay. Although small numerically, your religion is an indispensable factor in India's life. Parsis are among the best educated, the most industrious and the most cultured and charitable people of the subcontinent.

Parsis was a name given to those Persians who migrated to India a thousand and more years before the time of Christ, bringing with them the religion of the great seer Zoroaster, who lived, authorities say, six thousand years—some say six hundred—before the Christian Era. Whenever it was, Zoroaster, spokesman for Ahura-Mazda, is acclaimed by many historians as the seer of seers. You are often referred to as a Zoroastrian, though Parsi is the more accepted modern term.

There is something wondrously rich about the life and worship of your people: the bearded priests dressed in spotless white; the young scholars bending over the ancient holy books; the calm conviction of the adherents to your faith, the holy temples into which only Parsis are admitted; the Tower of Silence where your body will some day be solemnly laid after death, there to be devoured by the vultures; all are distinctive features of the religion of the inspired Persian prophet, Zoroaster. Always there is the temple fire, endlessly burning in its huge brass urn.

The temple fire is so holy that no non-Parsi is permitted to look upon it. Your people visit the temple almost daily, make their ablutions and proceed reverently to the place where the fire burns, there to say their prayers. They offer the priest a piece of polished sandalwood and he places it as an offering into the fire.

As the fire is fed, so also must you *keep your faith alive and burning by nourishing it with good thoughts, good words and good deeds.* Faith lives just as the sacred fire lives because the keepers of the temple sustain its holy flames with sticks of sandalwood, day and night, year after year. Faith, like the fire, demands constant care.

PREPARATION FOR THE FAITH

The formal introduction to your parental faith came when you were nine years old. For two years you had been preparing for a momentous childhood ceremony known as *Navajot*. You attended an out-of-doors school and learned your lessons under the scorching sun. Although some people say that Parsis are sun worshipers, you know they are not, even though you were taught to reverence the sun as a principle of life. Actually, during your school days, you considered the sun a rather fierce disciplinarian, equally as fierce as your bearded, priestly teachers. They stood over you with a stick, demanding perfection, especially in the prayers and recitations from the Avesta, the holy scriptures of your faith.

"Once more!" your teachers would say. "It must be like this," and they would demonstrate just how you were to accent *"Ashom Vohu,"* which meant "Most High God," with which almost every prayer began. Over and over you recited from the Gathas and the Yasts and the Vendidad, the ancient and difficult books of the Avesta.

Etched into your mind were the mighty sayings of Spitama Zoroaster; for example, his Golden Rule, which said, "That nature alone is good which shall not do unto another whatever is not good for its own self."

You knew that three strokes of the stick would be your punishment if you made one mistake, five strokes for two mistakes, and if you made three, you might as well beg for mercy. Those were the days you had your first struggle with Zoroaster's commandment about "good thoughts, good words, good deeds!"

"Let's break their sticks!" you would whisper when you got together with the other children. But sticks could easily be replaced.

"Let's run away!" But where would you go?

"Let's tell our fathers!" But you already knew that your father would tell you, as he always did, "Someday you will be grateful you had to learn the prayers and the holy words. And, remember, soon it will be time for *Navajot*."

Navajot. You did not know exactly what it would be like. No one told you the details. The bits of information you picked up from an older brother or sister were unofficial. All you knew was that whatever *Navajot* was, it could not be more demanding or more burdensome than all this training, this standing in the broiling sun by day or sitting under a smelly kerosene lamp at night, reciting at the top of your voice, mysterious and little-understood words such as, "When Ahriman came seventhly to Fire, which was combined against him, the Fire separated into five kinds, which are called the Propitious, the Good Diffuser, the Aurvazist, the Vazist, and the Supremely-Benefiting. And it produced the Propitious Fire itself in Heaven whose manifestation is in the Fire which burns on earth, and its propitiousness is this, that all the kinds are of its nature. . . ."

"Why must I recite so loud?" you once cried out. "Is God deaf?"

"No!" was your teacher's reply. "But *I* am!" And down had come the stick.

THE UNDERSTANDING OF GOD
BECOMES CLEARER

A week before *Navajot* your mother said, "Soon you will no longer wear the *zabhalan*." This was a sleeveless garment, a sack-like kimono, tied around the neck instead of the waist and worn by both boys and girls. You had looked forward to discarding it. On the day of *Navajot,* just before the ceremony, you would put it away forever.

Two days before *Navajot* a bearded priest came to your home. But this time instead of a stick, he carried candy and fruit. He was a jovial and happy man who filled the house with joy. "The days of learning are not over, my boy," he said, "but the hard training will now have its reward. *Navajot* is your day. You are the hero. You are God's chosen one. God wants you to be happy and free and share His love. You have no idea how quickly *Navajot* is passed and how soon one grows old."

After this he spoke long and tenderly about Zoroaster and of

how the Prophet had believed in one God, of how Zoroaster had
called God the King of Kings and how he had wished that all
the world would learn of His love. Then when the priest took
your hands in his and looked down at you with love and tenderness, your heart was singing. You could not understand why
there were tears in his eyes.

Your father, too, was something of a riddle to you during these
days. There had always been deep affection between you and
him, although you had known him as a stern man who, like your
teachers, demanded perfection from you. These days, however,
his voice was gentle and his thoughts seemed far away as he took
you aside and said, "So, my son, let me hear the prayers just as you
will say them at *Navajot.*"

You prayed and he listened with closed eyes. For the first time
the words you had learned mechanically took on a solemn meaning: "*Ashom Vohu!* I hereby make an attempt to ward off all evil.
Help me in my task. Oh, my God, I am your ardent follower. I
promise to live by all your precepts and I promise to be an ardent
Zoroastrian all my life. . . ."

When you finished there was a long time of quiet. Finally your
father opened his eyes and nodded as if to indicate you had
pleased him very much. Putting his arm around you, he said,
"You are my true son. I want you always to be my true son and
a loyal Parsi."

RELIGION IS A RITUAL

On the morning of the great day of *Navajot* at five o'clock,
the household was already stirring. You had just memorized what
you were to do. First there was the bath, during which your
mother poured milk and sugar on your body. Then you put on
the *zabhalan*—for the last time—and went alone into a room for
prayer. There would be no breakfast for you, not even a sip of the
customary tea, but there would be plenty to eat later—a feast, in
fact, in your honor. Like any boy of nine would have done, you
let your thoughts wander while you prayed, for you could not
forget that today you were, as the priest had said, something of a
hero. You were proud and excited to think that all the hurry and

the preparations, the singing of folk songs, and the sipping and sampling of wine were in your honor.

Soon the priest and your father came to you. "We are beginning with the small ceremony, namely *Nahan*," your father said. Then your mother came forward and taking your hand, led you to the door of the family bathroom where the ceremony was to begin. The priest asked you to stand before the door and face the east. There you stood; you in your *zabhalan* and the priest in his white garment. He began a prayer. You repeated it after him as perfectly as you could.

Then the priest asked you to extend your right hand and he placed into it a small metal cup containing a yellow liquid. You looked at him as if to ask if the liquid was really *nirangdeen*. You had heard of that, for it was the sanctified urine of the holy bull. In every large Parsi temple there is a courtyard where a great white bull is tethered. A sacred animal, he is kept spotlessly clean, a symbol of the creative power of God. The bull is not worshiped, as many non-Parsis believe, but like the fire, it exemplifies a spiritual truth, the power of procreation. Knowing all this, you were quite sure that you were holding the *nirangdeen*, even before the priest continued his prayers.

Fixing your eyes on the liquid and whispering several words of the prayer, you lifted the cup with both hands, remembering that you had been told that *nirangdeen* had the power to take away all the evil and sin which you had accumulated since birth. It was a purification. All Parsis believed and trusted in this mystery. So you closed your eyes and tipped the liquid into your mouth. Three times you drank until the cup was empty. After each sip, the priest handed you a pomegranate leaf which you slowly chewed, recalling that pomegranate is a symbol of everlasting life and that its leaves bring you the assurance of immortality.

A PARSI PURIFICATION

Then the priest and your mother took you into the bathroom for the purification. A spoonful of the sanctified urine of the bull was placed in the palms of your hands. You rubbed it over your face, over your arms from the elbows to your finger tips and from your neck down to your toes, covering every part of the body. After you had done this three times, you dried your body with a handful of sand. This done, your mother quickly washed your body with warm water and dried you with a towel. You took the lower half of a pair of white pajamas, a black cap and easy-to-remove sandals which she gave you to put on. The upper half of your body was left exposed. You then folded your *zabhalan* and though you had thought you would feel like throwing the childish garment away, you found yourself pressing it once more to your body as if saying good-by to a loving friend.

The priest then placed a cocoanut in your hands and escorted you to the verandah. Your relatives, forming a procession behind you, began to sing, creating an atmosphere of festivity all around you. Your mother, hurrying ahead, crossed the threshold leading to the verandah and waited there for you, holding in her left hand a tray on which were rice, a cocoanut, an egg and a pitcher of water. When you crossed the threshold—right foot first as you had been instructed—you waited while your mother took the cocoanut and then the egg and whirled them above your head three times. When she broke both the egg and the cocoanut on the left side of the threshold, everyone watched because it would have been an ill omen if the egg had been rotten or the cocoanut milk discolored.

Suddenly you realized that you were confronted with a large group of relatives and friends all looking up at you. As you approached a lovely carpet was unrolled at your feet and you remembered to step out of your sandals. Then you walked to the center area where twelve scholarly-looking priests were waiting. Dressed in white and wearing white turban-like caps, they reminded you of your teachers, but they were priests and they carried no sticks.

TODAY IS NAVAJOT!

In the center of the carpet was a low wooden dais, some three feet long and six inches high and covered with a pure white cloth. On the dais was an urn in which the symbolical fire was burning and from which rose the wondrous scent of the sandalwood. Nearby on a pedestal was a tray containing pomegranate seeds, almonds, cocoanuts, raisins and rice. Another pedestal held a large bronze tray laden with clothes and gifts.

The officiating priest escorted you to the cloth-covered dais where you were instructed to seat yourself, cross-legged. Into your hands the priest placed long strands of thread and a number of rupees. The twelve priests gathered around you as you sat facing the east. You remembered how your father had once told you not to look to the north during holy moments, for the north is the stronghold of evil forces, magnetic forces which disturb the mind and distort the influence spun by the priests as they intone their incantations. Their prayer was a chant which you knew so well that you repeated it with them word for word and pause for pause.

THE THREAD CEREMONY

Then you stood facing the east while the priest walked behind you and removed the white shawl from your shoulders. Placing a strand of thread around your neck, he let it hang down over your breast. As you recited the main prayer, the priest dressed you in the sacred shirt. First, he put on the right sleeve, then the left, and finally slipped the garment over your head. Gently arranging and smoothing this close-fitting white garment around your body, he took your hand in his as he continued the recitation.

He then took another thread, waved it three times to drive away the evil spirits and tied it around your waist. This was the greatest moment of all. The shirt would be your constant reminder that religion is a protective armor. The thread around the waist would be a symbol of the middle path, the path of moderation. The cap which you would later receive would signify spiritual adornment. But now the time had arrived for you to pray the prayer your father had so often heard you say, "*Ashom Vohu!* I hereby make an attempt to ward off all evil. Help me in my task. I am your ardent follower. I promise to live by all thy precepts and to be an ardent Zoroastrian all my life. The preachings and the practices of this religion are my only guiding rules."

Then you seated yourself on the white-covered dais while the priests gathered around you and the officiating priest recited a blessing and "sealed" you as a Zoroastrian with all the virtues and hopes of those who follow the Persian seer. As you heard this final pronouncement, you knew that never before had there been a day like this day and in a little while, there would be music and merrymaking all because of what was happening to you.

The priest's voice chanted on, but you had your own secret prayer, unlearned and unrehearsed. "O God," you whispered to yourself, "I never want to be in the bad pages of your book. I want always to wear the sacred shirt and the holy thread. A moment without them would be my greatest sin. They will always be next to me like my flesh and skin. I promise it to you, O friendly priest. I promise it to you, dear father and mother. I promise it to you, O Zoroaster and especially do I promise it to you, O God!"

You never wondered whether you could actually keep all the promises you were making. At this moment, you did not think about tomorrow. You only knew that Ahura-Mazda, God of the Parsis, who rules the world and watches over all His people, understood and accepted your prayer, for today was *Navajot*.

RELIGION IS A MATTER OF LEARNING

Had you been born a Parsi, your study of the faith would have continued for many years. But even with all your learning, you would have always found the teaching extremely difficult. That Zoroaster believed in one God long before the rise of monotheism in other faiths, that he preached about God's righteousness and love in days when the gods were still thought to be demanding and cruel, these were things you grasped easily. But that the great God Ahura-Mazda, somehow represented a good spirit called Spenta Mainyu as well as an evil spirit, Angra Mainyu, remained a mystery. Who and what were these conflicting heavenly beings? Were they sons of Ahura-Mazda in much the same way that Christians spoke of Logos and Lucifer? Were they entities or qualities or merely concepts? And if God was good, how could evil exist? These were questions which troubled you greatly as you continued your study in the beliefs of the Parsis.

RELIGION IS A STRUGGLE

The priests, however, seemed to understand these problems. Life, they insisted, is a matter of choice and there could be no choice if everything was good. But how could a good God create evil? Somehow he must have because Ahura-Mazda was continually saying to his children, "Choose ye this day whom you will serve." You often wondered about the Zoroastrian concept of good and evil principles or good and evil spirits. You were told that the warfare between right and wrong in men's hearts was also the world struggle. It was more. It was the struggle in the unseen world as well. Hosts of demons were continually contending against angelic hosts.

You concluded that evidently the great God Ahura-Mazda needed help. That was why your scriptures say, "When a person becomes fifteen years of age it is necessary that he should take one of the angels for his protection, one of the wise as his own sage, and one of the high priests as his own high priest."

Seeking further understanding in this problem of good and evil, you were introduced to the concept of the Amesha Spentas. These are said to be six holy spirits emanating from Ahura-Mazda. They are, in effect, personified influences of God readily available to man. You also learned that Ahura-Mazda, the God of Light, is opposed by Ahriman, the prince of darkness, and that the Amesha Spentas are opposed by demon spirits which are their evil counterpart. You now saw the struggle in the world and in life in terms of an equation, a battle line in which the forces were clearly drawn:

AHURA-MAZDA	opposed by	*AHRIMAN*
The Amesha Spentas:	" "	Demon Spirits:
Asha, knowledge of right and wrong	" "	*Druj,* false appearances
Vohu Manah, good mind or love	" "	*Akem,* temptation or evil

Kshathra, strength of spirit	"	"	*Dush-Khshathra,* cowardice
Armaiti, piety and faith	"	"	*Taromaiti,* false pretenses.
Haurvata, health and perfection	"	"	*Avetat,* misery
Ameretat, immortality	"	"	*Merethyn,* destruction

RELIGION IS A MATTER OF CHOICE

Your mission in life, as far as your religion was concerned, was becoming ever more understandable. You realized it would be necessary for you to resist the demons or evil spirits by summoning the Ameshas Spentas or good spirits to your aid. When you felt yourself beset by Evil (*Akem*), you would have to call upon the Good Mind (*Vohu Manah*). Or, if you found yourself overcome by *Avetat* or misery, you must quickly arouse *Naurvetat* or health and perfection to help you. Life, you learned, is a continual battle and you must ever depend upon your faith to help you. Life is a matter of choice in which a man can call upon either the god of light or the god of darkness. *The purpose of life is the attainment of good, but this attainment is meaningful only if evil exists, for in this way every man is called upon to exercise his choice.*

Had you been born a Parsi, you would have learned that this choice constitutes a law which says: If you follow that which is good, good is your reward; if you follow evil, you will be rewarded with evil. So you must continually pray for wisdom and seek, by every possible means, to determine what is evil and what is good.

Many years ago Zoroastrians were interested in occultism, alchemy, astrology and almost every form of mystery and magic which, they felt, would guide them in their quest for goodness and truth. Some Zoroastrians were known as Magi, highly skilled Persian mystics. Three of these wise men followed the star to Bethlehem, as modern Parsis now follow the light of truth wherever it may lead. As a Parsi you realize that there is much truth in Christianity and you are convinced of the greatness of Christ, but you believe that the surest guidance always came from

Zoroaster. He speaks to you in many ways, but most clearly out of the Pahlavi Texts, which tell about his life and death, and out of the Avesta, the scriptures which explain and confirm the teachings of your faith.

THE HOLY BOOKS, A GUIDE TO THAT WHICH IS GOOD

The Avesta teaches you that in order to be truly good, you need to be kind to all things: to people, to animals, to the earth and even to the thoughts you think. It says, "God created all creatures for progress, which is His wish; and it is necessary for us to promote whatever is His wish that your wish may be realized."

The Avesta reports that Zoroaster once inquired of God how he and his people might worship best and what manner of sacrifice they should make. Ahura-Mazda answered, "Go, O Zoroaster, towards the high-growing trees, and before one of them that is beautiful, high-growing, and mighty, say thou these words: 'Hail to thee! O good, holy tree, made by Ahura-Mazda! *Ashem Vohu!*'" Then Zoroaster was instructed to cut off a twig and hold it in his left hand, keeping his eyes fastened upon it and offer it to the fire while meditating upon the highest thoughts of goodness, beauty, and truth.

"Worship the earth," Zoroaster commanded his people, "worship the heavens, worship the good things that stand between earth and the heavens . . . worship the souls of the wild beasts and of the tame, worship the souls of the holy men and women, born at any time whose consciences struggle, or will struggle, or have struggled for the good."

THE AVESTA ALSO SPEAKS OF MARRIAGE

"He that hath a wife," says the holy *Avesta*, "is far above him that liveth in continence; he that maintaineth a household is far above him that hath none; he that hath children is far above him that hath no child."

Words such as these caused you to think about your own marriage when you reached a marriageable age. Parsis believe that next to a good education nothing is more important than finding the right partner in life, a partner who belongs to your country and most of all, to your religion.

Had you been born an orthodox Parsi, you would have tried to find an orthodox marriage partner; or if you were a reformed Parsi, whose beliefs are more liberal, you would have sought a mate among the reformed Zoroastrian group. Your religion allows first cousins to marry and such marriages are looked upon as propitious despite the biological threat of inbreeding.

You would also remember the "Square of Sanctions," which is a way of saying that in an ideal marriage all four sides or parties must agree. The four parties are: the girl's parents, the boy's parents, the girl and the boy. Parsis are very anxious to have their marriages turn out well and they know that it is difficult to secure a "Square of Sanctions" when one party is a non-Parsi.

When you talk of choice of partners you mean freedom of choice, but it is usually freedom within the Zoroastrian community. As a rule, Parsis have a dual system; either the parents choose the partner or the boy or the girl makes the choice. Both ways are considered valid. In olden times if a son wished to get married but lacked the courage to seek his own mate, he would drop some salt into his father's drinking water as a reminder that the father should begin looking around for a daughter-in-law. A girl, on the other hand, often confided her wishes to a friend, the friend conveying the wish to the girl's mother and thus the search for a marriage partner was begun.

MARRIAGE INVOLVES MORALITY

Somehow, just the right person was usually found and divorces among Parsis are practically unknown. The scriptures of Zoroastrianism have much to say about marriage and sexual relations and are tolerant towards wives who yield to temptation. One such reference in the holy books—the Vendidad—says, "If a man, knowing the woman's shame, wishes to take it off of her, he shall call together her father, mother, sisters, brothers, husband, the servants, the menials and the master and mistress of the house and shall say, 'This woman is with child by me.' And they shall answer, 'We are glad that her shame is taken off of her.' And the

man shall then support her and her child as a husband doth."
The same scriptures, however, are opposed to willful prostitution
or licentiousness and Zoroastrian morals are among the highest in
all the ancient faiths.

Had you been born a Parsi, you would have received much
counsel about morality prior to your marriage. The priest would
often have spoken to you and to your partner prior to the wedding
day, stressing the sanctity of married life, emphasizing the need
for living close to God and reminding you that you are to perpetuate in your children the cardinal Parsi ideals: *faith, wisdom,
and charity, the three great credentials of Zoroastrianism.*

"Worship together in your home," the priest would have told
you, "and your home will be a truly spiritual existence." He would
have impressed upon you that children are a man's richest blessings, a point that was established long ago in one of Zoroaster's
dreams. "I dreamed I saw a rich man without children," Zoroaster
said, "and he was not exalted in my eyes; and I beheld a poor man
with many children and he was exalted in my eyes."

MARRIAGE HAS ITS SYMBOLISM

On your wedding day, a garden spot would be festooned with
colorful streamers, a platform built and decorated, chairs set
out for relatives and guests and musicians engaged for the great
event. Two white-robed, turbaned priests would be in attendance.
Solemnly you and your partner would follow them to the platform where two chairs have been placed on either side of a white
curtain suspended from a wire to separate you from your marriage
partner. You would be able, however, to see the people, dressed
in their best, listening attentively while a priest questions both
of you on your marriage intentions. He wants to know whether
you will promise to lead an exemplary life, if you will love and
honor each other and be true to the teaching and the counsel
of the holy books.

Satisfied on these matters, he requests that you give each other
the right hand, which you do beneath the curtain. While your
hands are joined, the priest wraps a long string around your
hands seven times, continuing to wind the string seven times

around the chairs. Seven is a propitious number. There are seven chapters in one of the oldest Gathas, there are seven virtues and seven deadly sins, there are seven archangels before the throne of God and, of course, there are seven good and seven evil spirits vying for the souls of men.

Having finished winding the string around the chairs, the priest returns the ends of the string to your hands and ties a knot. Meanwhile, he has been chanting impressive passages from the Avesta. Then he speaks of the good life, of the struggle between good and evil and of the need for faith. When he has finished, he removes the curtain which has separated you and your mate. He explains that the bound hands are a symbol of spiritual union and that the bound chairs signify that religion will bind you forever to your home. So saying, be solemnly unwinds the thread.

Now you are each given a handful of rice and, at a signal from the priest, you toss these grains at each other, as a universal sign of a fruitful and prosperous life. The people, enjoying this little byplay, applaud while the musicians play briefly. This is the prelude to a sermon in which the priest dwells at length upon the five attitudes necessary for the good life: *innocence, discrimination, authority, reverence* and *steadfastness.* The service ends with a prayer and the time has come for the customary congratulations, gifts and the wedding feast.

Often, after this, when the priest meets you, he will say, "May the Amesha Spentas grant you honor among men through your offspring."

LOVE OF PEOPLE AND ANIMALS IS LOVE FOR LIFE

Your people are among the happiest in India. They are noted for the close fellowship that exists within the community of believers. They have a reputation for being industrious, highly moral and dedicated to the principles of their faith. They are also respected for their love for animals. In a country like India where everyone has been taught to reverence all life and where the cow is especially holy, there has, nonetheless, often been great neglect of animals, particularly of dogs and of beasts of burden.

No religious prophet spoke more clearly on this subject than did your prophet Zoroaster. Even Nietzsche, in his book, *Thus Spake Zarathustra*, (the Persian name for Zoroaster) pays tribute to the love the prophet had for animal life.

In the holy books Zoroaster reminds his people that, "In the ox is your strength and your reliance. In the ox is your victory; in the ox is your food and your raiment; in the ox is your tillage that causes food to come forth to you." And every Parsi knows the thoughtful tenderness with which Zoroaster spoke of dogs. "The dog has been created by God to be self-clad and self-shod, watchful and wakeful, sharp-fanged, born to accept his sustenance at the hand of man and to safeguard the goods of man. . . . Whoever shall strike a shepherd dog, a house dog, or a stray dog, or a hunting dog, when the soul of that man shall pass into the other world, it shall howl louder and grieve more sorely than the sheep in the forest when attacked by the wolf."

ANCIENT TRUTHS WITH MODERN MEANINGS

But if Zoroaster had much to say about animals, he had more to say about human life and how men should live. Commenting on temptation he said, "When an action or an opinion appears and one does not know if it be a sin or not, then, if it be possible, it is to be abandoned and is not to be done at all."

Speaking of sin, he declared, "God has given to all men sufficient ability to save themselves from sin as well as from the devil who is the source of their sins and woes."

Of rewards and punishments, he wisely proclaimed, "He who injures my possessions, from his actions no harm can come to me. The harm will return to him, to his own flesh, and will keep him far from the good life."

Few prophets spoke in more modern terms about healing than did Zoroaster when, thousands of years ago, he advised, "One may heal with the law, one may heal with the knife, one may heal with herbs, but among all remedies the best healing one is that which heals with the Holy Word; this one it is that will best drive away sickness from the body of the faithful; for this is the best of all remedies."

Zoroaster's words convince you that he was a man truly called of God. He walked among men like a messiah. Although little is known about his life, it is said that he was married three times, that by his first wife he had one son and three daughters and by his second wife two sons. He began his ministry at the age of thirty, confident that God had revealed Himself to him in visions and in dreams.

DEATH IS INESCAPABLE

Had you been born a Parsi, you would believe that Zoroaster came to show you not only how to live, but also how to die—nobly and without fear. You would remember his words when the hour came for you to embark on the great, mysterious adventure of immortality. "Fate has come upon me, it cannot be cast off. I come, O God, I rejoice, I submit!"

In keeping with Zoroaster's teaching, you would believe that after death your soul will be judged and rewarded according to the deeds, words and thoughts which were yours during this present life. You believe in heaven and in hell; the first as a place of loving fellowship, the second as a dark well of loneliness. Because heaven and hell are very real to you and because the destiny of your soul is all-important, you have learned a "prayer for the dying" as part of your religious training. You learned it so well you feel sure you can recite it even though death itself is waiting at your side: "I repent of all sins, all bad thoughts, all bad words, all bad deeds, which I may have thought or said or done in this world. O God, I repent of all these sins with all my thought, word, and deed, physical or mental, worldly or spiritual."

Your people take this confession with utmost seriousness, and you have seen men die peacefully because of the power of it. You have often gathered with your relatives when they prayed for the salvation of the departed during the three days following a death. You believe unquestioningly in the efficacy of prayers for the dead, convinced that the spirit of the departed hears and acknowledges both the confession and the prayers. Surely the Fravashis—the spirits of the ancestors and the holy angels who have ever watched over the one who has died—hear the prayers too and are now prepared to lead the liberated soul across the bridge of judgment. The ceremonies and prayers for the dead are intended to influence the Fravashis particularly, for their help is needed at this critical time. *But there is no fear of God among your people any more than there is fear of death.*

WHY THE DEAD ARE DEVOURED BY THE BIRDS

There is but one fear: contamination. Deep-seated in your mind is the belief that death gives the demon spirits a chance to use the corpse as a spawning ground for all sorts of evil and infection. To resist and counteract these influences, the holy books prescribe many important acts. The corpse must be washed and attired in a spotless, seamless white shroud. The sanctified urine of the temple bull must be employed to anoint the body of the dead. The ritual also suggests that a dog be momentarily brought into the dead man's presence, especially a dog with a spot above each eye which gives the impression of a four-eyed dog, for he will be a mystical guide for the soul during its pilgrimage after death.

Where shall the corpse be laid? When Zoroaster asked this question of God, God said, "On the highest summit, where there are always corpse-eating beasts and corpse-eating birds!"

The "highest summit" is the Tower of Silence or *Dakhma,* a lofty structure that looks like a campanile surrounded by gardens. Inside its circular walls is a section of stone slabs, open to the heavens, one for the corpses of men, one for women and one for children.

It is to these slabs that the corpse-bearers take the body. "Two men," says your holy scriptures, "strong and agile, having changed their garments, shall lay the body where there are the corpse-eating birds." To non-Parsis this may seem primitive and barbarous, but you know there is a deeply philosophical meaning behind the act. For it is believed among your people that the demon spirits have rushed into the corpse seeking to triumph over it. Instead, the birds of God's heaven triumph over the demons. It is a mystery which only you and your people fully comprehend.

You comprehend it, for you have seen the vultures soaring, waiting for their sacred prey and you remember how a devout follower of your faith once remarked, "When I give my body to the birds, this is my final act of charity."

You alone know the feeling of faith that floods your hearts as you stand with your people in the garden near the Tower of Silence. Only you know the depth of meaning when, on holy days, you look up beyond the Tower into the sky and say, "I repent of all my sins."

Some Parsis believe that some day the practice of disposing of the dead in the *Dakhma* will change and there have already been Parsi burials in the ground or in sepulchres above the ground. But custom is deep-seated and tradition is sacred. Therefore, because you have been taught that the dead body is contaminated, you would not defile the earth with it, nor would you desecrate the sacred fire by using its flames for the purpose of cremation.

The Towers of Silence still stand in India and the prayers of penance will continue to be repeated for countless years to come. In the ageless temples of Zoroaster the scent of the sandalwood still rises from the bronze vessels where the fires burn. The chants of the priests are still spoken in the old Avestan tongue and the holy books are still fondly read. "Holiness," says your scripture, "is the best of all good. Holiness is also happiness, and happy is the man who is holy with perfect holiness."

This is the ideal toward which you strive. This would be your creed, your hope and your faith, had you been born a Parsi.

3

Had You Been Born

a Buddhist

HAD YOU BEEN BORN A BUDDHIST, you would realize that your religion has unusual world importance, not only spiritually, but as a social force throughout Asia, India, China, Ceylon and Japan. It has also been introduced into America where its temples have been built in metropolitan centers, particularly on the East and West coasts. Of the 200,000,000 Buddhists in the world, some 85,000 are in the United States.

You would be the first to admit that Buddhism in America is different from Buddhism in Asia, that Buddhism in China is different from Buddhism in India, and that all-in-all your religion represents a maze of contrasts. But you would contend that all of the sects and groups in your religion in the various countries are linked together by a universally accepted "creed." You call it:

BELIEF IN THE THREE REFUGES

Throughout the realm of Buddhism, all of your people are united in this belief when they say, *"I take refuge in the Buddha; I take refuge in the Dharma; I take refuge in the Sangha."*

41

What are these Three Refuges? The first, of course is the Budda, the founder of your faith. He was an inspired teacher who lived some six hundred years before the birth of Christ. *When you say that you take refuge in him you not only mean the Buddha as a man, but you mean as well that the Buddha is a spirit and a consciousness, a state of mind and being.* For "Buddha" is a title meaning enlightenment or awakening. "I take refuge in the Buddha," means that you are confident that the enlightenment which was the Buddha's will guide you and help you in all your needs. You mean that you are identified with the creative source and power of the universe.

When you say, "I take refuge in the Dharma," you mean that you are trusting completely in the teachings and promises which the Buddha revealed. You mean that you are prepared to practice what he proclaimed and to demonstrate what he declared. You mean that the path of truth which he walked, the righteousness he revealed, the salvation or destiny which he promised are provable and real. Dharma is a process which, like the Hindu Karma, is based on an immutable law. It is faith in the law of cause and effect; faith in the universal principles which can be trusted as the basis of justice and love. *When you affirm that you take refuge in Dharma, you are saying that no matter what happens, no matter how unfair, unjust, or unreasonable life's circumstances may appear to be on the surface, you are determined to trust the unseen, sub-surface power that governs the universe and guides the world.*

The third Refuge, Sangha, means fellowship or communion. Specifically, it refers to the order of monks and disciples founded by the Buddha himself. But it means something more. *When you say, "I take refuge in the Sangha," you are testifying that there is a mystical fellowship of believers who are links in a chain of brotherhood and understanding.* Both the seen and the unseen congregation are bound together by the spirit of the Buddha. Sangha is that spiritual community whose influence molds and directs the destiny of men. When men worship together a power is generated, that is Sangha. When devoted followers of the Buddha, bound together by the quest for Buddha-hood, do the

Buddha's will and follow his teaching, one here, another there, unknown to one another, unseen by one another, that is Sangha.

When you begin your worship, kneeling or sitting before the little shrine in your home, the first words you whisper as an invocation are, "I take refuge in the Buddha; I take refuge in the Dharma; I take refuge in the Sangha." As you fix your eyes on the statue of the Buddha and breathe in the incense which reminds you of his teaching, you *sense* the Three Refuges. But when you intone your *dharanis* or *mantras* (words and syllables from the Sutras or holy writings), when you lay a flower on the shrine and see in it the hoped-for perfection of your own life, that is when you express the Three Refuges in your heart.

THE WORLD OF BUDDHISM

Often, when you have finished your meditation, you remain for a long time before the shrine and your mind reaches out to Buddhists everywhere. Your meditation on the Three Refuges brings the heterogeneous groups into a unified Buddhistic world. It is a colorful and dramatic world. It includes barefoot monks in saffron robes, who shuffle thoughtfully through ancient streets, carrying their clay bowls which are sometimes called "begging bowls." Many loyal Buddhists would not think of eating their first meal of the day without placing a token of food in a holy man's bowl. It is their acknowledgement of gratitude, their "grace before meals." This is Buddhism.

It includes thousands of other monks, also saffron clad. Monks called *phongyis* or *bhikkus* or *bonzis,* move among the people, live the life of religious men, reside in monasteries, teach in schools and do social service. Their shaved heads signify humility and discipline. They live by rules called the Vinaya, which bind them to a life of austerity. You see them bent over ancient texts, Pali texts, deciphering and interpreting age-old Sutras. You hear a scholar say, "Greatest of all is the Lotus-Sutra, for it teaches the way of salvation." And another answers, "Surely the Pajnapara-mita Sutras are greatest because they teach the true meaning of self." This is Buddhism.

You envision temples such as no other religion in the world can claim. In Rangoon, Burma, stands the Shwe Dagon whose forest of shimmering spires is covered with pure gold. Often, when a Buddhist dies, a loved one honors the departed by spreading a bit of gold leaf over one small section of these mighty towers, or a devoted follower shows his gratitude for some blessing received by performing such an act. Inch by inch, through hundreds of years, the patient, loving hands of worshipers have covered the massive pillars of the Shwe Dagon with imperishable gold. You remember the towering solid gold statue of the Buddha in Bangkok's Wat Bovornives monastery. You see again the giant, awe-inspiring figure of the Buddha in Kamakura, Japan and the unbelievably intricate carvings of the reclining Buddha in the Ajanta Caves in central India. You visualize the indescribably beautiful temples in Ceylon. All this is Buddhism.

As you sit before your shrine you are part of it, part of the monastic life, the teachings, the temples. You are part of the three-fold belief: the Buddha, the Dharma, the Sangha. Over and over you tell yourself, "Buddhism is not divided! It is one invincible faith founded on the Three Refuges."

LAMAISM—THE BUDDHISM OF TIBET

Had you been born a Buddhist, you would know that, among non-Buddhists, there is great misunderstanding and misinformation about your religion. Take, for example, Buddhism in Tibet. For more than a thousand years, Tibetan Buddhism has been a mystery shrouded in the awesome mists of the Himalayas, romanticized by writers and glamorized by weird tales filtering through forbidden monastery walls. Out of Tibet came stories about prayer wheels endlessly turning, of haunting Tibetan horns continually being blown to frighten away evil spirits and of temple gongs eternally echoing in shadowy rooms plated with gold. When people talked to you about your religion, they wanted to know about Tibet. Was it true that there were oracles and soothsayers there who could look into the future? Were there, high up in that fabulous spiritual retreat, strange monks who could leave their bodies and magically span the earth?

What could you reply? Like most members of your faith, you were reluctant to say just what some Buddhist adepts *could* achieve during periods of meditation. Strange and wonderful things *did* happen in Buddhism and no one had ever exhausted the full power of the mind or the mystery inherent in deep meditation. Tibet was a mystery, even to you, but it was not a "queer" country nor was Buddhism in Tibet all mystery and magic. It was a philosophical approach to life based upon the belief that a true realization of self can come only if a man frees himself from the desires of the flesh and attachments of the world.

THE DALAI LAMA

You would know, however, that Buddhism in Tibet is actually Lamaism, a religion of priests who practice many rituals and make up an hierarchical organization with the Dalai Lama at its head.

You would be familiar with the Communist invasion of Tibet and the flight of the Dalai Lama. Escaping with a hundred of his devoted followers, this spiritual leader fled to India in 1960. The non-Buddhist world and the press described the Dalai Lama as just another man, not unlike other religious figures, a mortal man subject to the circumstances of life just as all men are. But to many Tibetans he was a god or the incarnation of a Bodhisattva, one of that group of chosen souls who prefer to live on earth and help people rather than to live, if they wished, in heaven. He ruled like a king and it was believed that no force in heaven or on earth could ever dislodge him; yet he, even as many others, fled before the guns and planes of the invaders.

The Dalai Lama had a rival, called the Panchem Lama, and their rivalry was fully as political as it was religious. When the "Red invaders" came to Tibet, it was said by some authorities, that they drove out the Dalai Lama and set up the Panchen Lama in his place. Other reports maintained that the Dalai Lama fled for fear of his own safety, relinquishing the field to the Panchen Lama. But no matter what actually happened or who may be right, it is your belief that both the Dalai Lama and the Panchen Lama believed in the Three Refuges: the Buddha, the Dharma, and the Sangha.

BUDDHISM IN CHINA

Buddhism in China has had a glorious history ever since the first century A.D. At that time, according to legend, Emperor Ming had a wonderful dream. He saw a man whose body was covered with gold step out of the blazing sun and stream down to earth like a golden ray. He saw him conquer the world with his beauty and the challenging power of his thought. Astrologers interpreted the dream by saying, "Surely this golden man is the Buddha!" So the emperor requested that the Buddha's statue and Buddhist priests be brought from India to China to teach his people the Buddha way of life.

The people of China interpreted Buddhism as a religion of renunciation because monks and priests pledged themselves to live according to the three monastic vows: *poverty, defenselessness, and chastity*. Many Buddhists in China who became vegetarians, refused to kill any living thing. Others spent their entire lives in meditation. But in all their practices they never set absolute rules or prohibitions for their followers. Buddhism, they insisted, made every person responsible for his own acts and it urged every individual to find peace and tranquillity within himself and for himself.

China followed Mahayana Buddhism, a theistic form, whose devotees adhered to the ancient Sanskrit texts. Mahayana was a philosophical approach to life that permitted adjustment to ever-changing political scenes. It was referred to as the "greater way" to distinguish it from Hinayana, a non-theistic and almost entirely monastic form of faith whose scriptures were written in the Pali language. Hinayana, also called Theravada Buddhism, flourished in such countries as Thailand, Laos, Burma, Cambodia and Ceylon, while Mahayana claimed China, Korea and Japan. Wherever Buddhism spread, it soon developed groups within groups and sects within sects. But wherever it was established, whether in the most remote Himalayan retreat or at the shrine at which you worshiped, the faithful follower always said, "I take refuge in the Buddha; I take refuge in the Dharma; I take refuge in the Sangha."

GOD AND BUDDHISM

Not much was said about God as far as your faith was concerned. Any concept of God was beyond man's grasp and since Buddhism was a practical approach to life, why not deal with practical things? India, where Buddhism was born, had so many Hindu gods that no one could number them. They were often made in the image of men, but Buddhism was made in the image of concepts, great concepts about life and how life should be lived. If the truth were known, you often tell yourself, Buddhism has no God in the Hindu or Christian sense, nor does it have a saviour or a messiah. It has the Buddha. And he was the Enlightened One, the Shower-of-the-Way.

The Buddha! His name as far as you are concerned is above every other name, yet you do not worship him. You worship *through* him. Through him you find your own true nature, the nature of reality and your relationship with all of life. You have a statue of the Buddha to help you in this awareness. Many Buddhists do not believe in statues and you secretly wonder whether the Buddha himself would not be a bit displeased if he returned to earth and found statues and images of himself. But just as people have pictures of their loved ones to remind them of their nearness, so you feel it is right for you to have an image of the Buddha.

Some Buddhists even say that the life of the Buddha—the Buddha as a man—is unimportant. They emphasize that it is only his message and his disciplines that are important. But often, as you meditate, as you sit before your shrine perplexed about life's problems and wondering how other people come to terms with them, you find inspiration in the story of the Buddha as a man. For you believe that the soul of the Buddha lived in heaven from the beginning of time, waiting for the moment in which it was to reveal itself to the world. And you may wonder whether your soul lived in heaven before it came to manifest itself on earth.

It is not quite clear just where and what heaven is, but you believe that somewhere there is a realm of emancipation, a state of bliss and a oneness with reality that underlies all life. You have a name for this state of "non-existent-existence"; you call it Nirvana. While Nirvana is a kind of heaven, it is, even more, a perfect blending with the essence of life. You believe that some-where, somehow, the spirit of the Buddha was waiting in a Nirvanic realm, waiting to be born as a man.

THE BIRTH OF THE BUDDHA

In the year 563 B.C., the Buddhistic soul, the Bodhisattva, entered the body of Queen Maya, wife of King Sudhodanna Gautama who ruled the Sakya clan in the Himalayan valley of the Ganges in India. The annunciation came to Queen Maya in a dream. She dreamed that a magnificent white elephant descended from the skies and entered her body. She told her dream to the wise men in the king's palace and they said it meant that she would give birth to a son who would be either a great emperor over a temporal kingdom or a great teacher over a spiritual world.

While waiting the birth of the child, Queen Maya decided to visit her parents in the village of Devahrada, but along the way she heard a voice warning her that her son would be delivered before she reached her parental home. Seeking refuge, she retreated into Lumbini Park. Reaching up to support herself by holding to the branches of a tree, she discovered that the tree miraculously bowed down as if to worship her. Here, alone, and yet sustained by a great power, she gave birth to Prince Siddhartha Gautama. At that very moment seven other births took place in the Sakya kingdom: five male children who were to become Buddha's disciples; a baby girl who would one day be his wife; and a horse which was also to become important in the unfolding of the drama of Prince Gautama, the foreordained Buddha.

When Queen Maya returned to the palace with the child, the king and his people staged a great celebration. The young prince was taken into a Hindu temple for consecration. There three Brahman wise men repeated what had already been proclaimed: the child would either be an emperor or a teacher at the age of thirty.

THE BUDDHA'S BOYHOOD

King Sudhodanna, concerned over the prophecy that his son might some day abandon the throne, vowed to shield Prince Siddhartha from the world. The king had been warned by astrologers that if the prince ever became aware of the suffering in the world, he would surely try to help mankind through spiritual rather than material aid. Therefore, the king commanded his subjects never to let Prince Gautama be exposed to either the sight of sorrow or the presence of death. And so it was that within the kingdom walls Prince Gautama, living in a sort of make-believe world and enjoying a sort of make-believe peace, saw only the happiness of his father's court.

During this sheltered existence many miracles took place in the life of the young prince. These are part of the Buddha legends and you, as a Buddhist, see in them psychological truths, although some people take them literally. One story relates that one day the prince fell asleep in the shade of a tree and although the shade of every other tree shifted with the sun, the cool shadows never changed at the spot where Prince Gautama lay. Another account tells that, at the age of twelve, he confounded his teachers with his superior knowledge. At sixteen he so distinguished himself at archery that he won the right to marry his cousin Yasodhara who, as has been said, was born connaturally on the day of his birth.

For twenty-nine years Prince Gautama was spared the sight of suffering until one morning he drove into a city in his horse-drawn chariot. There he saw an old man wearily making his unsteady way along the road. The prince was confronted for the first time with the tragedy of age. Then, in quick succession, he saw a sick man bowed down with disease and a dead man being carried to the waiting funeral pyre. These three scenes revealed to Prince Gautama the true nature of suffering. Here were the agony of age, the tragedy of disease and the sorrow of death; from one or all, no living soul is spared. It was a divine drama and it plunged the prince into deep sadness. He was never to forget what he had seen, nor could he forget the contrast which he observed in the face of a serene and peaceful monk who quietly made his way along these same streets. Surely the monk had found the answer to life's riddle. Surely the man who had set his heart on self-discovery would find peace.

Prince Gautama was never the same after this experience. Haunted by his thoughts, he finally made a tremendous decision. He determined to give up his wife, his only son, his parents and his kingdom and resolved to walk throughout the world as the monk had done. He would search for the answers to the question of suffering and pain. This was to be his mission. This was why he had come into the world.

THE GREAT RENUNCIATION

Thus, one night, a night which you and all Buddhists still refer to as the Night of the Great Renunciation, Prince Gautama left his father's house. In a chariot, drawn by the horse which had been born on the same day that he had been born, the Prince started toward the tightly barred palace gates. As the horse approached, the gates mysteriously opened of their own accord. The prince and his charioteer rode through, out into the world.

Carrying neither money nor food, the prince proceeded deep into the forest where he shaved his head and put aside his royal garments to don the lowly garb of a monk and to begin his pilgrimage. The charioteer, after vainly trying to dissuade him, returned to the palace. Here, confronted by the royal family, he told them the story, witnessed their consternation and then in anguish, died of a broken heart.

Such is the legend of the Buddha, from his advent to his renunciation of a worldly kingdom. Such is the narrative of the prince who became a beggar and entered into his "hidden years" at the age of thirty. Then the story continues, telling how he studied with Brahman priests, how he walked observingly in the world, how he shouldered the burdens, the sorrow and the pain of the people and unceasingly sought for wisdom.

HOW DOES A MAN RECOGNIZE HIS OWN DIVINITY?

Was he aware of his divinity? Did he know throughout his wanderings that he was the Buddha and that his spirit was the spirit of Eternal Consciousness? You are not sure. There are some things about your faith you cannot answer decisively. There are too many speculations among your people for you to be arbitrary about many things. As a devout Buddhist you realize there are three kinds of truth: *absolute truth, relative truth,* and *illusory truth.* Buddhism, you contend, is always reasonable in its points of view, Buddhism is willing to speculate on all questions of life and that is why you are reluctant to say decisively that Prince Gautama knew he was the Buddha before he became the Buddha. Does every man know whether he, himself, is divine? Who is to say that every man is not a potential Buddha?

As you worship before your shrine, you know that for you Buddhism holds great meaning. You remember how, when you were four years old, you had been initiated into Buddhism in an impressive ceremony. Your head had been shaved, you were given the garb of a monk and you had carried a begging bowl for part of a day. The ceremony was to impress upon you the influence of the Buddha. Many of your boyhood friends became monks at the age of nineteen or twenty because they wished to continue the special religious life which had been impressed upon them when they were four. Girls often became Buddhist nuns.

The most wonderful part about Buddhism, you believe, is that it helps an individual to experience what the Buddha, himself, went through in his life. This is what the priests in the temple tried to make clear to you during the ceremony and later, during your school years when you were taught by Buddhist monks. *Buddhism is a religion of teaching.* There are no sacraments, nor elaborate ritual; no redemptive plan, nor promise of heaven or hell, no doctrine that man is conceived and born in sin. *Buddhism is an awareness.* It is belief in the Three Refuges: the Buddha, the Dharma, and the Sangha.

If you feel sometimes that there is a miraculous force at work in your life, you recall that this too was part of the Buddha's experience. Although Buddhism lays no stress on miracles, there are wondrous legends about the founder of your faith. Once he tossed a rice bowl into a river and it floated upstream. On another occasion a pile of straw on which he prayed was transformed into a beautiful altar. Gods, disguised as devils, tempted him, offering him the kingdoms of the world if he would but bow down and serve them, but he refused. All these things are links in a chain of remembrances that must surely have led the Buddha back to a realization of the heavenly abode from which he came and sometimes during your meditations, you have the feeling that your soul, too, was once a Bodhisattva living in heaven since the beginning of time.

The true awareness of who and what the Buddha was came to Prince Gautama through prolonged meditation. For seven weeks, in fasting and prayer, he sat beneath a Bodhi-tree (the pipal or sacred fig tree), determined not to rise until he had solved the problem of suffering and the mystery of pain. Here in Bihar, India, deserted by friends, weak from hunger and longing, he received his illumination. It was as if he relived the endless cycles of cause and effect existent since the beginning of time. He gradually saw the world of truth unfold for him. His mind was opened. A light surrounded him. He discovered that the cosmos and he were one, and it was at this moment that he realized his Buddha-hood.

THE BUDDHA AND YOU

Had you been born a Buddhist, you too would see yourself under the Bodhi-tree. You would also wish to make the discovery that your leader made. You would believe that your true Self is God and that God is the true Self—although even as you said this, you would substitute the term "Universal Consciousness" for "God."

Self with a small "s" is mortal, subject to pleasure and pain, responsive to life's highs and lows, bombarded by change, wrecked by the three tormentors: age, sickness, and death. But all of these occurrences, while appearing real and important to self, are immaterial to the higher Self. True life, according to Buddhism, is a superconscious life, and in this you admit there is a close parallel to the Christian concept of "dying unto self" in order to realize the Christ within.

THE BUDDHA AND CHRISTIANITY

Had you been born a Buddhist, you would recognize many similarities between Buddhism and Christianity. Although the Buddha is in no way a messiah, as was the Christ, he came to save men; not from sin, as Jesus had done, but, rather, from *nature* by demonstrating that nature is an unreality. The Buddha gathered his disciples around him and preached his "sermon on the mount" at what is now Sarnath, India. Here, in a deer park called Isipatana, he related what had been revealed to him throughout his pilgrimage and during his meditation under the Bodhi-tree.

"Hear, O my disciples," he said, "I will explain to you the truth of suffering, the cause of suffering, the end of suffering and the way that leads to the end of suffering. Birth is suffering; old age is suffering; sickness is suffering; death is suffering; sorrow, lamentation, dejection and despair are suffering. Contact with unpleasant things is suffering. . . . And these are the causes of suffering: the craving for pleasure and lust, the craving for passion, the craving for existence, the craving for vanity. . . . Now, the cessation of suffering is to cease from attachment. Attachment originates in craving, and craving originates in ignorance. To cease from suffering, cease from attachment; to cease from attachment, cease from craving; to cease from craving, cease from ignorance. . . ."

So spoke the Buddha to his disciples and having captured their minds with his logic, he now proceeded to capture their hearts with his love. It was all very well to talk of suffering and the cessation of suffering, and it was reasonable to warn people that they must "cease from craving, cease from ignorance," but how could this be done in actual practice? The Enlightened One had an answer and had you been born a Buddhist, you would hold it as a cardinal creed. The answer lay in what the Buddha himself called the Eightfold Path. It consisted of:

1. Right views
2. Right intention

3. Right speech

4. Right action

5. Right livelihood

6. Right effort

7. Right mindfulness

8. Right concentration

The Buddha also referred to these eight principles as the Middle Way, and he meant that a man should live moderately between extreme spirituality and extreme secularism. This, he felt, was a rule which all people should follow. "My doctrine," he said, "makes no distinction between high and low or between rich and poor. It is like the sky. It has room for all; and like the rain, it washes all alike."

For forty-five years he preached and lived his gospel. For nearly half a century he went about doing good, telling his disciples, "Let your light so shine before the world that you, having embraced the religious life, according to our well-taught doctrine and discipline, may be seen by men as possessing forbearance and meekness."

He established Five Great Commandments:

1. Do not kill

2. Do not steal

3. Do not commit adultery

4. Do not bear false witness

5. Do not abuse your body with strong drink.

He was not interested in final answers. His mission was to turn men's hearts from fruitless speculation into a way of life. His aim, he said, was to lift men above themselves or out of themselves into a higher consciousness where they could realize the greatest potential of their spiritual natures. When someone asked him, "Where is heaven?" he replied, "Walk the Eightfold Path." When he was prodded by those who wanted to know what the soul was like and how and in what form a person would live again, he told them, "Let that which I have not revealed remain unrevealed."

"But, Master," asked a disciple "of what does religion consist?"

"It consists," the Buddha replied, "in doing as little harm as possible, in doing good in abundance, in practicing love, compassion, truthfulness and purity in all walks of life."

So spoke the Buddha and shortly before his death, he called his disciples around him and said, "Go now, O monks, and wander for the benefit of the many, for the welfare of mankind, out of compassion for the world. Preach the doctrine. If it is not preached to men, they cannot attain salvation. Proclaim to them a life of holiness."

There were many likenesses between Buddhism and Christianity, but there was also one major difference. Buddhism did not believe in salvation through a messiah, a redeemer, or any person. It believed in salvation through oneself, meeting one's own problems, exonerating one's own sins, and finally, facing death itself with a supreme confidence in Self.

THE DEATH OF THE BUDDHA

In a grove of trees, near the holy city of Benares, India, where he had spent his years of ministry, the seventy-five-year-old Buddha clasped the hand of his best-loved disciple, Ananda, which means the blessed one, and told him not to weep. "Whatever is born," explained the Buddha, "bears within itself the seed of dissolution. Impermanent are compound things. Work out your salvation with earnestness."

Had you been born a Buddhist, you would often meditate upon the death of the Buddha because you knew that your life, too, carried within it the "seed of dissolution." Where would you seek help? In the Three Refuges: the Buddha, the Dharma, the Sangha. And what happens after death? Buddhists are divided in their opinions. Some, like the Lamas, believe that the mind guides the life essence into another stage of consciousness. Others, like the Mahayanas, believe that a process or an energy is reincarnated in another life, perhaps on this planet, perhaps elsewhere. Hinayana or Theravada Buddhists often cremate the body, keeping the ashes in an urn somewhere in their home.

The Buddha was buried, though no one knows exactly where. Relics of his body, including the famous tooth of the Buddha in the Temple of the Tooth in Kandy, Ceylon, began to be revered. It was said that miracles took place in the stupas and pagodas where these relics were enshrined. You wonder whether this would have been the Buddha's wish, even though, as you know, entire cities—like the one at Pagan, Burma, once built to honor him—were later abandoned and reduced to ruins by the ravages of time.

The Buddha's words and the Buddha's teaching, you feel, are far more important than stupas and pagodas or even cities. His philosophies and sayings, collected after his death and assembled into scriptures called Pitakas (which means baskets), are the true treasures of your faith. The sacred canon of Buddhism contains three such "Baskets" and they are called Tipitaka or Tripitaka.

THE HOLY BOOKS OF BUDDHISM

The first Basket is known as the Vinaya-Pitaka, a book of rules for the various orders of monks and nuns. It contains the history of how the disciplines and the orders were formulated, how these should be enforced, and what the Buddha had to say about them in his sermons and discourses. The second Basket is the Sutta-Pitaka or book of sermons containing the gospel according to the Buddha. It records the Four Noble Truths:

1. The truth of suffering

2. The cause of suffering

3. The cessation of suffering

4. The way that leads to the cessation of suffering

It also explains the Eightfold Path and offers instructions in the form of dialogues between the master and his disciples as well as a summary of Buddhist ethics under the title of the Dhammapada. The third Basket is the Abhidhamma-Pitaka and is called the "Basket of Development." It discusses Dharma, the way of life, and the cause and essence of all living things.

There are also other writings, such as the Jatakas, comprised of more than five hundred legends; they deal with accounts of the Buddha, many of which are supposed to have taken place in his previous incarnations. It is believed that the soul of the Buddha may have manifested itself many times before he came to earth, just as it is believed that he has, no doubt, reappeared many times since he died, perhaps even as a Jesus or a Mohammed or some other famous personage. But the greatest thought among all of the writings is this: "I take refuge in the Buddha, I take refuge in the Dharma, I take refuge in the Sangha."

THE SECTS OF BUDDHISM

As you worship before your shrine, secure in the Three Refuges, you feel as though you were in the very center of the stirring world of Buddhism, a world which, you insist, is based on equality and justice. It is a world which has never denied admittance to anyone, no matter what his race, color, or station in life may have been. Around you are many "Buddhas" or, rather, the Buddha as known by many names, such as: Sakyamuni, the historical Buddha; Amida, the Buddha of eternal light and life; Avalokitesvara, the Buddha of love and Kevannon, the Japanese Buddha of mercy. Around you is also the great galaxy of Buddhistic expressions represented in more than forty schools of thought, all claiming to be truth and all, apparently, able to prove their claim to the satisfaction of their followers.

These many "denominations" bear ambitious names: Tendai (salvation for all); Nichiren (named after its thirteenth century founder); the Mystical School (a pantheistic approach to universal understanding); the Shingon School (a school of mystical enlightenment); the Hsuan-tsang School (named after its seventh century founder); the Pure Land School (a pietistic sect of the Mahayana movement); and many more, including the group which has captivated the attention of America: Zen Buddhism.

Zen, you tell yourself, although a highly mystical expression of your faith, is not as rational as Buddhism usually is. Its exponents, however, would be the first to say it is one of the most practical and reasonable of all the groups and sects. *Zen seeks to help men realize the universality of the Buddha nature in themselves, in the universe, and in the living essence of all life; but, most of all, it seeks universality in the interrelation of all three.*

Zen is neither easy nor simple. In Burma, the form of the word is Zan; in India, Jhana; and in Japan, from where it spread to America, it is Zen. The Burmese Buddhist uses Zan as a very mysterious and profound process to attain supernatural powers through concentration. He strives to attain trance-like states, to study color absorption, and to develop various degrees of meditation which eventually lead him to perform supernormal acts. Indian Jhanas resort to yoga practices in an effort to enter a state of bliss called Samadhi. But the Japanese believe that the aim of Zen is to return man to his true form of being and to recognize that that form is formless.

Zen does not believe in institutionalized expressions of Buddhism; it has no set pattern, and it will have nothing to do with the deification of the Buddha. "If you meet the Buddha, kill him," says a Zen teacher, by which he means not only that the Buddha never wished to be worshiped, but that there is an awareness greater than Buddha-hood, the awareness found through abstract meditative practices.

The founder of Zen was Bodhidharma, who was born about a thousand years after the Buddha. He not only opposed the formalism that had grown up around the Enlightened One, but he was disturbed by the cults that presumed to re-interpet the Buddha's teaching. "Religion," said Bodhidharma, "has but one goal: the direct realization of truth. Anything that interferes with this must be swept away."

"Let us not be concerned about the *way* toward the goal of truth," said this reformer. "Let us be concerned only about truth. Every act, every thought, every impulse is your religion. Do not talk religion; do not argue religion; do not teach religion; just *experience* religion."

Zen grew out of the deepest possible interpretation of the triple

Refuge: the Buddha, the Dharma, the Sangha. It surrounded itself with stories and paradoxes in an effort to find and teach
"truth." It ridiculed people who thought they were being religious
when they merely talked about religion, or monks who imagined
themselves Buddhas because they sat under Bodhi-trees, or people
who said they could not worship unless they had just the right
temples and priests. It said that a man can be a spiritual being no
matter what his occupation or place in life may be and no matter
where he may live or worship. *The faith of every man has already
been planted in his consciousness,* said Zen.

Soon people were devoting themselves to *zazen* (ascetic meditation) seeking to achieve *satori,* a state of enlightenment. They
began employing philosophical problems called *Ko-an* on which
they meditated. These required a high degree of "intuitive reason-
ing." A favorite *Ko-an,* so popular it soon became a cliché, pro-
posed, "If clapping two hands makes a sound, what happens if you
clap one hand?"

Zen stories caught the popular fancy and many people
claimed they found some deeply hidden truth in them. "Once
there was a pilgrim who came to a Zen and said, 'I want to find
the Buddha.' The Zen, who was drawing a bucket of water out of
the well, pulled it up slowly hand over hand. When he got it to
the top of the well, he poured the water over the pilgrim's head.
Frightened, the pilgrim cried out, 'Why did you do that?' The
Zen replied, 'It is just as sensible for me to pour water on you as
it is for you to ask me to show you the Buddha. If you must ask
where the Buddha is, no one can tell you.'"

Another story told how two men came to a river where a lovely
girl was afraid to cross. The older of the two men picked her up
and waded through to the other side where he set her down and
she went her way. The two men walked on together all day, saying nothing. Toward nightfall the younger of the two spoke.
"Brother," he said, "I do not think it was proper for you to carry
that girl across the stream." The older man answered, "Brother, I
carried her only for several moments while crossing the water.
You have been carrying her all day."

All this is Buddhism. From Lamaism in Tibet to Zen in the

United States, the Prince who became a beggar left a profound impression upon the world even as he inspires you to meditate before your shrine. As he challenges the world, so he challenges you. His voice and his words seem as real to you as though you had lived with him during the days of his ministry. His image will be before you in the dwindling light of your old age. Although the incense on his altar will burn low, what he represents to you will become ever clearer as the years go by.

THE BUDDHA'S LIFE IS THE LEGEND OF EVERY MAN

"I, too," you tell yourself, "was born in a 'palace,' the child of a king, as was the Buddha. I, too, came into the world bearing with me something of the divine. Protected for a while from the full impact of the world, I was never quite inspired to think about my destiny and the meaning of life until I saw, as did Prince Gautama, the manifestation of suffering, sickness and death from which no one is spared."

Like the young Prince, you must seek to recognize your Buddha-hood. You must learn that nothing is permanent. Your heart must be fixed on eternal, not on temporal, values. You must realize that to do good is the greatest joy; to love peace is the highest motive; to live as though this life is but part of an onward-going life is the deepest truth a man can ever find. And what is the greatest law by which a man can live? The Buddha called it not a law but a golden rule. He said, *"Hurt not others with that which pains you."*

Had you been born a Buddhist and were you seated in the shadows, alone before your shrine, and were you to think about the Buddha's golden rule, you would wonder if, perhaps, his faith has been made more complex by his followers than he ever intended it to be.

You must keep uppermost in mind the truth that realization of self can come only if a person frees himself from the desires of the flesh and the attachments of the world. There is a technique in Buddhism which tells you how to meditate. It says that, as you sit quietly before your shrine, you should visualize a cup of muddied water. It is muddied because it has been shaken and disturbed, but as it is quieted, all the murk and sediment go to the bottom. Then the water becomes clear. It is suggested that a man's mind is like that cup of water, and it is the silence of meditation that induces the mind to be stilled and cleared.

Sometimes it seems to you that Buddhism itself has been muddied; time, political discord, and theology have caused it to be so involved that its simple beauty and directness have been obscured. Yet, as you journey back through the maze of meanings and clear away the trappings with which the Buddha has been enmeshed for 2500 years, you stand face to face with yourself, your true self, made in the image of what the world calls God.

Then when your mind is stilled, when you wonder how you can more fully realize that Self and hold to it and truly walk the path your Founder trod, you know there is a way. It is found in the threefold Refuge: the Buddha, the Dharma and the Sangha. Knowing their deepest meaning you can live at peace, and die, as did the Enlightened One, in the knowledge that dying, too, is a part of life.

Such would be your faith—had you been born a Buddhist.

4

Had You Been Born
a Confucianist

Had you been born a Confucianist, you would be a member of a movement which was never intended to be an organized religion. You would adhere to a system of opinions which was not designed to be regarded as scripture. You would be following a man who had no desire to be a messiah, a prophet, or a saint.

There are followers of your faith wherever there are people of Chinese descent, whether "overseas Chinese" in Taiwan and southeast Asia, or Chinese in the Americas. But the chances would be ten-thousand-to-one that you would be living on the Chinese mainland where the great majority of the world's 320,000,000 Confucianists live. That vast and sprawling Asian continent now called the People's Republic, which westerners refer to as "Red China" would very likely be your home.

It is not Red China to you even though a red flag with five stars flies over it and even though you and your 650,000,000 fellowmen are Communist controlled. You do not see your nation through western eyes. You see it through the turbulent flow of history, the history of your homeland; a nation which is and always will be known to you by its native name, *Chung-Hua Min-Kuo*, the oldest empire in all the world, the largest republic in all the world, and the dynasty of the world's most venerable sage: K'ung-fu-tze (Confucius).

CONFUCIUS AND YOUR COUNTRY ARE INSEPARABLE

Confucius is not only a man and a legend; he is also the spirit and the hope of your people and your land. Born nearly 600 years before the time of Christ, he grew up in the village of Chow which is in the state of Lu and in the province of Shantung. Even today many refer to the province as holy ground.

There is a question as to whether Confucius' mother, Ching-tsai, was officially married to Shu-liang Ho, the military officer who was to become his father, or whether she was his concubine. There are also conflicting stories about her age. Some authorities say she was fifteen; others, seventeen, when Confucius was born. But all agree about the age of Shu-liang Ho; he was in his early seventies when he met Ching-tsai. Even though he had already sired nine daughters by his first wife, and one son, a cripple, by a mistress, the virgin Ching-tsai accepted all this because of her love for Shu-liang Ho.

History has it that they prayed together for a son at ancestral shrines and that they went together to sacred Mount Mu to offer sacrifices and to plead with all that is holy that they might be blessed with a healthy child. The answer to their prayers was Confucius, born on an autumn day in 551 B.C.

There is also the legend which relates how, during her pregnancy, Ching-tsai had a dream. One night a rare and fabulous animal, the *chi-lin*, part-tiger, part-dragon, whose function it was to announce the coming of kings, appeared to her. In Chiang-tsai's dream, the *chi-lin* prophesied that her child would be born in a "Hollow Mulberry Tree."

As this was the designation for a certain cave in the vicinity of Chow, Ching-tsai went there to await the birth of her firstborn.

Unattended, she brought him forth while two benevolent dragons stalked the skies, putting the power of evil to flight, and while five of the planets, disguised as ancient sages and guided by a voice from heaven, circled the holy place of birth. Later, when she carried her son into the village to their home, the trees bowed down in worship to the young mother and her child.

Had you been born a Confucianist, you would accept both the man and the legend. You would also accept the spirit and the hope embodied in what Confucius represented in the life and history of your people. You would enter into the sentiments of your most noted historian, Ssu-Ma Chi'en who, writing in the first century of the Christian era, said, "While reading the works of Confucius, I have always fancied I could see the man as he was in life, and, when I went to Shantung, I actually beheld his carriage, his robes, and the material parts of his ceremonial usages. There were his descendants practicing the old rites in their ancestral homes; and I lingered on, unable to tear myself away."

That is how you feel today as you live and move among the rapidly shifting scenes in your teeming nation. The hope and the spirit of Confucius are always there, just beneath the surface of the visible life. And although the old ancestral homes are reluctantly giving way to a new era, you know that he is still walking with his people through the triumph and the pain of change. He was a peripatetic teacher like Plato and Socrates, a seeker of the Way, like the Buddha. He was a philosopher not unlike his countryman, Lao-Tze, whom he met but once. To those who knew him, he was the immortal sage.

Sometimes he rode in a bullock cart while his students walked alongside. He had the wit and the wisdom they needed, and he lived the kind of life they felt stirring within themselves, a life which, they believed, could remake men and remake their country, too, and help both to realize their greatness.

The heart of this greatness was, according to Confucius, "true gentlemanliness." That was his touchstone; what would the true gentleman be like, what would he do, how would he act, what would be his highest aspirations and his major concerns? Confucius found the perfect image of the perfect man among the divine sages and the valorous heroes of the past. Actually, they may never have existed except as archetypes, but for Master K'ung these men were real. He believed that they lived just beneath or within the surface man. To him, they represented an idealized past through which he hoped to create a perfect present. But how was this to be done? Through many things and in many ways. Through the true recognition of one's duties, through knowledge, through ritual, through respect for one's ancestors, through an awareness of one's potential and most of all, through love, which is Tao, the Way.

With such ideals Confucius lived and by these rules he taught, never proudly, never feeling that he had attained, and never boasting about his own achievements. He was a happy, yet a lonely man; a knowledgeable, but a searching man; a tranquil, yet a frequently disturbed man; a humble man, convinced that there were others more humble; a wise man, confident that there were others more wise; a man of uncommon sensitivity, who drew unto himself the heart of every other man who ever felt the divine discontent in his own unfulfilled life.

"Many," said the historian Ssu-Ma Chi'ien, "are the princes and the prophets that the world has seen in its time; glorious in life, forgotten in death. But Confucius, though only a humble member of the cotton-clothed masses, remains among us after many generations. He is the model for such as would be wise. By all, from the Son of Heaven down to the lowliest student, the supremacy of his principles is fully and freely admitted. He may, indeed, be pronounced the divinest of men."

CONFUCIUS AND YOU

If you could hear the rumble of your Master's bullock cart today, you would no doubt be walking beside it. Your respect for Confucius is that great. It is as great as that manifested in one of his disciples, Yen Hui. This young man, separated from Master K'ung during a riot in a city, was reunited with him only after a considerable period. Confucius said to him, "I thought you had died." And Yen Hui replied, "While you are alive, how should I dare to die?"

Had you been born a Confucianist, you would often say the same, "How can I die while the spirit and the dream persist; the spirit of what the Master taught—gentlemanliness, and the dream he inspired—a society of gentle but superior people living together in righteousness and truth?"

You met Confucius first in your parental home. Because of him you were taught quietness and reverence for all things. You were reminded that you should respect all life, that you should be observant and courteous. Even in little things, the presence of Confucius seemed to stand over you. You never discarded paper upon which Chinese calligraphy appeared or where the printed word was used, for this would have been a mark of discourtesy. Politeness, filial piety, love were part of the Confucian tradition. His *yen yu* (words that work) were implanted in your mind as part of a folk tradition, as part of a philosophy, and as part of a living faith.

You were taught his Golden Rule: "What you do not want done to yourself, do not do to others."

You were instructed in his definition of love and wisdom: "What is love? To love mankind. What is wisdom? To know mankind."

You memorized his counsel to youth: "Youth, when at home, should be filial, and when abroad, respectful to his elders. He should be earnest and truthful. He should overflow in love to all and cultivate the friendship of the good."

You never forgot his challenge to goodness: "If you really want goodness, you will find it at your very side."

You understood his insight into learning when he said: "Learning undigested by thought is labor lost; thought unassisted by learning is dangerous."

Confucius and you grew up together, united, not separated, by the more than 2000 years that stretch between your lives. Often when you hear the rumble of a bullock-drawn cart, you imagine Master K'ung as he sat in the jostling vehicle, amused at himself that he should occupy such a make-believe throne when he knew it was but a lowly traveling school. He also knew that no matter how far he went or how long he traveled, he would never catch up with the ancient sages of the land he loved: those men whom he created in the image of his dreams.

He was a player on life's stage re-enacting their ideals, and within the drama were truths enough to feed a hungry heart for all its life. Even when he was a boy, he gathered other lads around him and directed them in the presentation of the rituals for the dead. They would make believe they understood the symbolism of the ageless Chinese forms, the winged dragons and the personified planets. With utmost seriousness, they played their divine games while their elders, watching, began to wonder how all this hidden knowledge had been revealed.

Confucius said that he learned it at his mother's knee. He had lost both his parents when he was quite young, for his father had died when he was two years old and, when his mother died, while he was in his teens, the make-believe ritual of his childhood became a reality. He observed a three-year period of mourning with strict observances of the amenities of ancestral worship. "When parents are alive," he told his companions, "they should be served according to the rules of propriety. When they are dead, they should be buried according to the rules of propriety. After they are buried, they should be honored and sacrificed to according to the rules of propriety. . . . Though a man may never before have revealed his true self, he is certain to do so when mourning for a father or a mother."

Such counsel, passed by oral tradition from generation to generation, found its way into print and became part of your heritage. In fact, your most important training for life was by way of the *Five Classics,* books which Confucius distilled out of the religious lore of the Chinese ancients and to which he added his own insights into the meaning of the spiritual life.

Like hundreds of millions of Chinese who have come and gone since Confucius walked the earth, you, too, have been favored as one to whom he spoke from the pages of these treasured writings: *The Book of History* (Shu Ching), the emergence and progress of your nation from 2357 to 627 B.C.; *The Book of Changes* (I Ching), an esoteric study devoted to divination, symbolism and

oracular sayings; *The Book of Rites* (Li Chi), a study of ceremonial forms; *The Book of Poetry* (Shih Ching), a collection of
more than 300 songs, odes and ballads; *The Book of Spring and
Autumn Annals* (Ch'un Ch'iu), events in the state of Lu before
and during the period of Master K'ung.

Later you were introduced to the Confucian scriptures, commonly known as *The Four Books*. Here were the renowned
Analects (Lun Yu) or conversations of Confucius; *The Book
Mencius (Meng-tze)*, which holds the teachings of Master K'ung
as seen by his most famous interpreter, Mencius; *The Doctrine of
the Mean (Chung Yung)*, a catechism of Confucian teaching
prepared by the grandson of Confucius, K'ung Chi; and *The
Great Learning (Ta Haio)*, a treatise on the proper conduct in the
life of the individual, the family and the state. That is how
Master K'ung became your teacher and how he seemed almost
like an ancestor and a parent to you.

THE DEIFICATION WAS INEVITABLE

Because millions of your countrymen long before your time felt
as you did about this nearness to the master teacher, they made
the sage a savior quite against his will. They built temples and
shrines to honor him and if there should ever be a state religion
in your country, it would be founded upon the life and the
sayings of Kung-fu-tze.

Even though the red flag may have cast a shadow over religion,
and Communism may have persuaded many people that speculation about the Way of Heaven is a sign of immaturity, your
temples are open and public gatherings to Confucius are carried
on. His birthday is still observed on September 27 and his spirit
is still your people's spirit and their dream.

His deification, represented in temples and in special festivals, is
first of all an attitude in the human heart, for that is where
Confucius lives. Form and ritual, he insisted, must always contribute to an enrichment and an improvement of life. Unless
they do, they are empty and meaningless. "In the morning," he
said, "hear the Way of Heaven; in the evening, die content." He

spoke with the wisdom of the mythological seers who were his models and it was inevitable that his apotheosis should eventually take place.

It began even before Master K'ung departed this life. It was in the making whenever the bullock cart lumbered through a village street. It was hastened every time one of his 3000 students or one among his 72 superior scholars said, "I have met the Master and he spoke to me." But it was in the summer of the year 479 B.C. that his canonization took recognizable form. Because he was ill, it was hinted that the time of his demise was near. Despite his seeming indifference to fame, he confessed concern that after his death he would soon be forgotten. "The path which I have laid out," he murmured, "will soon be obscured by weeds and grass. How then shall I be known to posterity?"

Foreshadowings of his departure deepened his concern. There was the occasion when a hunter came to him and asked if Master K'ung would kindly identify a mysterious animal which the hunter had killed. Because it was a strange and frightening beast, he had dragged it to a rubbish pile and there discarded it. The hunter was so concerned over what he had done that he had come to see the wise sage, hoping that at least he could tell him what it was.

Old Confucius took his staff and walked laboriously with the hunter to the refuse heap. There lay a lifeless animal which appeared to be part-tiger, part-dragon. Confucius stood looking down upon it, his wrinkled hands steadying his trembling body on his staff. He shook his head in anguish. "It is the *chi lin,*" he said. "But why was he slain? Or why has he appeared at all at such a time since he is supposed to come only when kings are to be born?"

He worked doubly hard after that, seeking to complete his *Book of Spring and Autumn.* He worked as though the hunters with their guns stood over him. When the book was finished, he summoned his best-loved disciple, Tze K'ung. The weakened Master dragged himself despairingly back and forth across the courtyard of his home.

"Why are you so late?" he asked Tze K'ung. "The sacred mountain is crumbling, the roof beam is breaking, the old sage is withering away."

Tze K'ung whispered, "If this is true, to whom then can I go?" Because of love for him, Confucius wept.

EVEN THE WISEST OF MEN MUST DIE

Had you been born a Confucianist, you would realize how often your path crosses the path of Master K'ung as you try to cope with the world in all its many phases. How great his wisdom really was! How quickly his maxims find response in your heart!

You visualize his meeting with Tze K'ung, how Confucius retired to his chamber, and how he sat alone prepared to entertain his final guest: Death. What thoughts passed through his mind? Once he had said, "When people want you and need you, go to them; when they set you aside, then hide." Age and a changing world had set him aside as he reached his final hours. Perhaps he wanted to hide, not only from people, but also from death. Did he dread to die, you wonder? Hardly. He had often said, "Heaven has endowed me with what I am, what have I to fear?" Confucius, teacher of gentlemanliness and shower of the Way, seemed to be always honest in his counsel and harmoniously attuned with his teachings.

Perhaps, there in the shadows, the "crumbling mountain" looked back across the winding path over which he had come in his seventy-seven years, looked back all the way from the "Hollow Mulberry Tree" to the darkening edge of an ancestral tomb, from the *chi-lin* which had announced his birth to the dead *chi-lin* in the refuse heap. He must have seen, as does every man, the passing sequence of life and have felt the truth of his words, "He who seeks nothing more than a bit of rice to eat, a bit of water to drink, and a bent arm for a pillow, he will, even without looking for it, find happiness."

Along memory's path he caught glimpses of the boyish rituals which he had instigated, then his marriage, a not too happy one, and the birth of a son and a daughter. Then there were his careers: first, that of a tithing master who recorded the tenants' grain for their feudal lord, then the keeper of a granary, then an administrator of public works, then Grand Secretary of Justice in the state of Lu, then Chief Minister, but in every position he was always the teacher, devoting himself to the development of gentlemanliness in himself and others.

"True manhood," he insisted, "consists in realizing your true self and in restoring universal virtue. Whosoever will realize his true self and restore universal virtue, the world will follow him."

But the world did not follow him. The world did not learn of him. The world did not become virtuous. "Why are yóu so late, Tze K'ung?" he had said to his faithful disciple, and this must have been what he felt like saying to the world, "Why are you so late, O world? Why are you so late?"

Born a Confucianist and living on the Chinese mainland, you would share not only the old Master's concern but occasionally his tears. For your country, no less than many other nations, is late, so very late in believing in the wisdom of the Master. As in the days of Confucius when the dukes and the lords fought for power, so governments and war lords are fighting for power in your time. And as the people 2500 years ago were reluctant to adopt his teachings, even though his teachings had worked when sincerely tried, so today they are still being rejected of men.

The "gospel" of Master K'ung did work indeed. It worked so well for a short time in the state of Lu that people said, "We have seen what paradise is like." In that brief Confucian period, love was really love and justice was really just. There was a saying that theft ceased to exist among the people because it had been removed from people's hearts. An era of trust and mutual faith had been ushered in. The good of one was premised on the good of all. Anything lost on the highways was restored, and any wrong was righted because gentlemanliness was man's richest prize. In those days Confucius said, "The superior man understands what is right; the inferior man understands what will sell."

The utopia did not last. The Prince of Lu, in whose employ Confucius served, fell from grace. It happened that the neighboring state of Ch'i, concerned that a miracle in morals had taken place in Lu and fearing that its people would soon be moving to the "land of Confucius," set out to prove that all states are vulnerable. The Baron of Ch'i sent a harem of beautiful dancing girls as a gift to the Prince of Lu. In due time, despite all efforts on the part of Master K'ung, the Prince was neglecting his observances of both "state and church." "I have never yet," said Confucius, "found anyone whose desire to build up his moral power was as strong as his sexual desire." So saying, he resigned and, for a time, left the state.

"Government," he declared, "consists of the correct choice of officials. One must elevate the just men so that they can exert pressure upon crooked men, for in this way the crooked may be made straight." But he saw that the crooked again had become crooked because the straight had become crooked. And the old sage demurred that the saddest thing about the world is the fact that "virtue is not cultivated, that knowledge is not made clear, that people hear of duty and do not practice it, that those who know they are evil do nothing to improve themselves."

"A gentleman," he concluded, "is one who is at least troubled by his shortcomings."

You hazard the guess that these were some of the things that Confucius thought about as he sat in the shadows awaiting his final guest, looking back over the years of his life. And you wonder again what his thoughts would be if he were walking your nation's streets today.

His sovereign sayings hint at an answer, "From life to death is man's reach," he said, which seemed to infer that there is nothing which a man cannot conquer if he will but conquer himself.

"What is wisdom?" he had asked, and then had answered his own question by saying, "It is to know mankind. And what is love? It is to love mankind."

How shall one meet the inevitable? "Wade the deep places, lift your robe through the shallows."

And if that is not enough, then, "Keep your will on the Way

of Heaven, lean on the mind, rest in love, and move in art."

"But, Master," you say, "now that you must die, what do you think? Do you believe that you will live again in a life to come?" And you remember how Confucius said, "We do not yet know about this life. How then can we know about death?"

And so he died, as a gentleman, attended only by a grandson and several of his disciples, chief among whom was Tze K'ung. They performed the solemn rites and buried him on the bank of the River Szu. Ironically it was the Duke of Lu—who was anything but a gentleman—who ordered that a song of mourning be composed in which he said, "Merciful Heaven, surely thou hast no compassion upon me, for thou hast not left me the one aged man fitted to protect me, the Unique One, during the period of my rule. Full of mourning am I in my pain. O woe! Father Ni! Now I no longer have anyone who can serve me as a model!"

If the old Master heard the song, he no doubt shook his head and said, "Why are you so late?"

THE CONFUCIANISM OF CONFUCIUS

Had you been born a Confucianist, you would realize that the institutionalized form of your religion is closely interrelated with the destiny of your country. So are the other traditional religions in China: Taoism and Buddhism. There are also some 50,000,000 followers of Islam and approximately 4,000,000 Christians, mostly Roman Catholic, but since the advent of the Communist regime (1949) foreign religions and foreign missionaries have no longer been tolerated.

You are often bewildered as you seek to appraise the Chinese religious scene. You are permitted to maintain your home altar where a small table inscribed with the name of Confucius holds a prominent place and where you observe the amenities of meditating on the good life. You may also worship at the ancestral shrines where the soul tablets of older generations are preserved and you may honor the individual graves with your sacrifices. *In many homes, a tablet on the altar depicts in artistic ideograms: Heaven, Earth, the Rulers, Ancestors and Confucius.* You may worship here or you may go to the temples if you wish, but you know that the consensus of government officials is against such practices. Communism opposes any and all religions, philosophy, or ideology which are not in conformity with Marxist views.

Open opposition to Confucianism is demonstrated by your Communist leaders in many ways. The printing and the distribution of *The Five Classics* and *The Four Books* have not been ordered stopped. Atheistic teaching has not succeeded in subverting the immortal sage or reducing his teaching to folk tradition. Confucius is treated by the Communists as an historical figure important in Chinese history. Wherever his teachings agree with Marxist views, his teachings are endorsed. But the spearhead of opposition is the creeping propaganda which is directed against all religions in an attempt to persuade men that religious idealism and religious practices are a sign of immaturity and that respect for spiritual traditions is wasteful superstition.

Determined to make an objective evaluation of Confucianism's true merits, you are being driven more and more to an investigation of the intrinsic value which it embodies for you and your world. You wish to discover with absolute certainty what there is in Master K'ung that, under the pressure of modern circumstances, you will be willing to live for and if necessary, die for. You wish to be fully convinced of its truth. Your faith, assaulted by a dynamic, authoritarian force, is on trial and you know that if it is to endure, it must recover an equally vital dynamism within itself.

You do not find this dynamism in the temples or even in the Confucian cult which perpetuates the ceremonials; neither do you find it in the outward forms or in the emotionalism with which some adherents approach the faith. All such expressions, you feel, are vulnerable and could be submerged by a powerful secular state. What can never be conquered, however, is the "Confucianism of Confucius" by which is meant the understanding of human nature in its relationship to divine nature, a concept so ancient and so deep-rooted that it represents the very essence of your people's life and thought.

It often seems to you that Confucianism in this sense might profit from the threat of communism by putting its house in order.

For Confucianism, as a temple cult, had fallen into a sterile formalism long before Marxism unfurled its red flag over your republic. Many Confucian temples were in disrepair and in disrepute generations before Communism came. They had become little more than museum attractions. Rituals had been neglected, precepts were ignored and the way of gentlemanliness was ridiculed as the ghost of an unrealistic past.

Now, however, under the harsh intrusion of a regimented rule, a rule which reaches down into every ancestral home to disintegrate that home and into every individual life to dominate that life, thoughtful people are becoming introspective and are re-examining the depth and sincerity of their old beliefs. They are searching not only for the meaning of existence, but are relating this meaning to the divine wisdom of their neglected sages, particularly the wisdom of Master K'ung.

You, like others of your faith, looking back into the past, hoping to find a way for the future, realize that more than 3000 years *before* Confucius, your ancient mentors speculated that life has purpose inherent in itself and interconnected with powers beyond itself. Man's recognition of this union was considered a decisive factor in the development of the individual. One of the earliest of the sages, Yu, who lived in 2000 B.C., said, "Follow what is right and you will be fortunate; do not follow it and you will be unfortunate; the results of life are but the shadows and echoes of your acts." The holy Tang, an equally ancient seer, declared, "It is Heaven's way to bless the good and to bring calamity to the evil."

Confucius, the spiritual protégé of such men, became the Master who formulated these concepts into a philosophy which fulfilled the needs of a people who were innately questing by nature. His religion encouraged man's search for dignity, man's search for the highest possible social order and man's determination to come to terms with the universe which is his "cradle and his grave." Confucius, motivated by the conviction that each individual is dependent upon the other and that all are dependent upon Heaven, came with the simplest of all messages—a message built upon a single word, *jen,* a synonym for all that is good. It was *jen* that Confucius saw as the secret and elusive ingredient which transforms men and gives rise to a new-born social order. The manifestation of *jen* in the individual projected itself into society as universal virtue or *li*. *Li* is many things: it is ritual, it is protocol, it is a rod that means "give room to others." According to the Master, *jen* was perfect manhood, *li* the perfect social consciousness.

Jen and *li*, like the hypothetical sages whom Confucius dramatized in his illustrious sayings, are conceivable but perhaps unrealizable ideals. Like the ancient zodiacal light, seen fleetingly in the west at twilight and in the east before dawn, *jen* and *li* might be, for most men, no more than a mirage of goodness, but for Confucius they were real. *Jen* was the logos of the gospel he preached and the life he lived; *li* was the "holy spirit" of his teaching in the world.

When you are sensitive to the needs of others, that is *jen*. When you are good in a world that is evil, that is *jen*. When you are honest at a time when it would seem to be expedient to be dishonest, that is *jen*. Whenever you seek to realize your highest nature, that is *jen*.

When you do not raise yourself above your fellowmen or lower yourself because of them, when you walk without pride in your achievements and without remorse because of your limitations, that is *jen*. *Jen* is the heart and soul of gentlemanliness; *li* is the spirit of gentlemanliness universalized.

The Master said, "A gentleman takes as much trouble to discover what is right as lesser men take to discover what is profitable."

"In the presence of a good man, think of how you may learn to equal him. In the presence of a bad man, turn your gaze within."

"A gentleman in his dealings with the world has neither enmities nor affections. Wherever he sees the Right, he seeks to identify himself with it."

"The demands that a gentleman makes are upon himself; those that a small man makes are upon others."

"Clever talk and a pretentious manner are seldom found in *jen*."

"The gentleman is one who takes the right as his material, and ritual as his guide in putting into practice what is right."

"In private life, courteous; in public life, diligent; in relationships, loyal." That is *jen*.

The harmonization of our moral being with the universe; that is *li*.

Although Confucius made no reference to a personal God, he did teach about the over-ruling *Tien*, the immutable force to which men and society are subject. Reluctant to discuss the possibility of man's immortality, he, nonetheless, endorsed the ancient and noble tradition of ancestor worship. Deprecating the need for prayers, he never ceased to urge himself and others to live every moment as though Heaven were watching. Heaven to him, as to all Chinese, was but another name for *Tien* or God. Thus, religion for Confucius embraced philosophy and philosophy embraced religion, and as you review the Confucianism of Confucius, one thing remains clear: the person who dedicates himself to goodness finds his place in life and fills it, and by so doing he fulfills himself.

THE DISCIPLES OF CONFUCIANISM

As the ancient sages linked Confucius with the historic past, so the Master's disciples formed a living bridge between his era and the present. This "apostolic succession" began in earnest when his disciples came to pay their respects at his grave on the bank of the River Szu in the state of Chow. They observed the traditional three years (twenty-seven months) of mourning, and the Duke of Chow offered cattle and sheep sacrifices, as was the custom.

Tze K'ung dramatized his personal grief by building a hut near his master's grave and living there for the remaining six years of his life. Following his example, almost a hundred other admirers of Master K'ung did the same, some building shelters large enough to house their families. A village called K'ung-lin grew up, a ceremonial hall was dedicated, and Confucianism rapidly became a cult.

Meanwhile, the disciples became masters in their own right, re-interpreting, redefining and all too frequently, paraphrasing and altering the words of Confucius to fit their personal and pre-conceived ideas. Every step hastened their Master's apotheosis. His writings were canonized and his legends became the basis for divinations. His death day was made a time for rituals and sacrifices, and his birthday a holiday marked with ceremonial extravaganzas. Temples, shrines and halls of learning rose across the land and as was bound to happen, sects sprang up, each claiming omniscience in interpreting the Master's will.

Among the votaries none was more like Confucius than his disciple, Men Tzu (Mencius), although he lived only thirty-nine short years (371-289 B.C.), he made his life an imitation of his Master's in both thought and deed. Like Confucius, Mencius stressed the quality of *jen* as the hallmark of true manhood and of *li* as the credential of an acceptable social order. To *jen* and *li*, he added "righteousness" as the supreme virtue of the Way, and the belief that man himself is a symbol of the universe. Like Confucius, he immortalized the ancient seers and with them as his models, he, too, traveled from state to state as Confucius had done, trying to persuade rulers to try the great experiment: the governed will reflect the conduct of their governors. "Goodness," said Mencius, speaking as Master K'ung had done, "must have its source in the rulers themselves. If not, where will the people go for their contemporary examples?"

He was no more successful than Confucius had been in changing the rulers' attitudes, and eventually he confined himself to the task of enshrining *jen* and *li* in his disciples. In this he seemed to excel. Those who made up the Mencius school became, for a time, the true Confucianists and after Mencius died, he was mourned and revered even as Confucius had been. His disciples, too, compiled his sayings with affection. They became teachers in their own right and developed, as Mencius had suggested, schools of meditation.

Then the elements of *Yang* and *Yin*, the positive and negative forces in the universe, became identified with Confucianism, giving it a cosmological emphasis. Later, neo-Confucianism made the role of reason ever more important in the growing tenets of the faith and more schools of thought arose. Neo-Confucianism had its disciples in such scholars as the statesman saint, Wang An-shih (1021-1086), the idealist Ch'eng Yi (1033-1108), the reformer Chu Hsi (1130-1200), the mystic Lu Chiu-yuan (1139-1193) and others. Meanwhile, a new gospel of eclecticism sprang up within the movement, bringing an ever greater amalgamation of Taoism, Confucianism and Buddhism into evidence. Often such an approach, hailed as a religion for the masses, spread itself so thin that it drifted into nothingness or everythingness, depending upon the point of view.

Master K'ung would hardly recognize his teaching or his disciples were he to return to the "New China." He would not only find his teachings encrusted with a rigorous theology and his simple sayings coldly encased in complex rituals, he would see that superstition, legend and mythology are intermingled with a critical rationalism in a hard-to-identify approach to faith. Most of all, he would discover that in the religion called by his name, the goal is to worship the messenger instead of seeking to live his message.

Witnessing Communism's advent, he would, no doubt, feel, as you often do, that perhaps Marxism is the nemesis in China's religious history and that a living faith is desperately needed if a people are to survive.

TO BE REMEMBERED IS TO BE IMMORTAL

Confucius is the example. When you see your old way of life slowly disintegrating under a new political and social order, you turn with thoughtful sincerity to your immortal sage. You find him beside you in every emergency and in every new, forbidding crisis. Riding in his bullock cart, he is with you as you walk searchingly through the loneliness of crowded city streets.

He lives in your heart as the realist: "I do not expect to find a saint today, but if I find a gentleman I shall be quite content."

. . . . . as the humanist: "They who know the truth are not

equal to those who love it, and they who love it are not equal to those who delight in it."

. . . . . as the counselor: "In the presence of a good man, think of how you may learn to equal him. In the presence of a bad man, turn your gaze within."

. . . . . as the mentor: "If I were to select one phrase to cover all my instructions, it would be, 'Let there be no evil in your thoughts.'"

. . . . . as the balanced man, "To exceed is as bad as not to reach."

. . . . . as the mystic, "One should sacrifice to a spirit as though the spirit were present."

. . . . . as the statesman, "If you govern the people by regulations and keep order among them by chastisements, they will flee from you and lose all self-respect. Govern them by moral force, keep order among them by ritual, and they will keep their self-respect and come to you of their own accord."

. . . . . as the man of insight, "In old days men studied for the sake of self-improvement; nowadays men study in order to impress other people."

. . . . . as the perfect sage, "Without goodness a man cannot for long endure adversity, nor can he for long enjoy prosperity."

You loved him for his sense of humor, "There is no need to think thrice before acting. Twice is quite enough."

You knew him as one who was ever sensitive of others. It is said that when, at a meal, he found himself seated next to someone who was in mourning, he did not eat his fill, and that when he wept at a funeral, during the rest of the day, he would not sing. It was told how he would fish only with a line but never with a net, and that when he went hunting he would never aim at a roosting bird.

You feel about Confucius as Yen Hui must have felt when he said, "The more I strain my gaze up towards the Master's moral character, the higher it soars. The deeper I bore down into it, the harder it becomes. If I see it in front of me, suddenly it is behind. Step by step the Master lures me on. He has broadened me with culture and restrained me with ritual. Even if I wanted to stop, I could not. Just when I think that I have exhausted every resource, something seems to rise up, standing out sharp and clear. Yet though I long to pursue it, I can find no way of getting to it at all."

Confucius and your country continually merge in your mind. They are so intricately related, so equally loved that to lose one is to be deprived of both. Only if you *live* Confucianism, you tell yourself, can you pay your debt to Master K'ung and to the China he so dearly loved. You are embroiled in a great conflict, this battle between his China and your China, between freedom and force, between faith and fear. But where, better than in your land, should these lines be drawn and these issues decided? Could it be that Master K'ung had something like this in mind when he said, "New rulers never come to a land but by Heaven's decree?"

Could he have meant that rulers come not always to bless but sometimes to purge? Could he have known that in the purging, the man of true gentlemanliness might rediscover himself, amend his ways, and turn once more for strength and truth to God? And if man does do that, what then? Will Heaven rush to his aid, and somehow, in a way not known or seen by ordinary men, project its power in such a way that goodness itself will triumph though all has seemed as lost?

Such would be your thoughts—had you been born a Confucianist and were you living in the China of today.

5

Had You Been Born
a Shintoist

Had you been born a Shintoist, you would find it impossible to separate your faith from your fatherland, Japan. Japan, for you, is Shinto, and Shinto is Japan. Almost all of the world's 60,000,000 members of your religion live on these islands. Here are its 20,000 Shinto priests and its more than 100,000 Shinto shrines.

Japan is the Land of the Rising Sun, a descriptive term which grew out of Shinto. Here, where you were born, Shinto was born, a religion without a holy book, without creeds, without sacraments, and, in the beginning, without a name. It was originally a way of thinking, a way of looking at life, and when a name was needed it was called Shinto, which means the Way of the Gods.

REMEMBER THE WORD: KAMI!

The Shinto liturgical year is built around many important festivals. There are also Sunday services in many temples and shrines, but the most important function of the shrine is the opportunity it affords for personal, private meditations. You go to a shrine whenever you feel the need for special spiritual help. Most of all, you go to pay your respect to the *kami*, the deities of Shinto. *But kami are more than deities or gods in the ordinary sense; they are the essence of life.* Some people may think of them as angels or celestial beings of one kind or another, but while *kami* may mean all this, you always remember that *kami* is a life force, a power complete in itself and yet a manifestation of universal power. *Kami* is a spirit. It is also a principle or principles of all that constitutes love, justice, rightness and order among men and in the universe.

In olden times each class of people, each trade, each vocation, had its *kami*. There were the *kami* of carpenters, shopkeepers, farmers, politicians, and many more. It was believed that proper respect and worship of these *kami* assured good fortune, expert artistry, and successful achievement. But even so, people were also convinced that their own effort, as well as their devotion to the *kami*, influenced their destiny. In this way the *kami* were something like the Hindu Karma, the law of cause and effect. A Shinto teacher, trying to clarify this rather complex idea, once said, "*Kami* is an honorific term extolling the sacred authority and sublime virtue of spiritual things, and all things are spiritual."

Your mind dwells on the *kami* as you walk through the groves surrounding the shrines. The lovely landscaping, the exquisite flower gardens, the well-tended trees, especially the holy *sakaki*, a verdant evergreen, remind you that the *kami* have breathed life and beauty into everything on earth. The earth, says Shinto, is a reflection of heaven; and man is God externalized.

Had you been born a Shintoist, you would find a great lesson in these peaceful groves. Although your religion does not pretend to be philosophical, it does provide the answer to many puzzling questions. When you ask, "What is it that makes a tree put forth its branches, all different, yet all alike? Why does a tree reach a certain height and then grow no higher?" The answer is, "It is the *kami* within the tree fulfilling itself. It is the *kami* working out its destiny and its purpose."

THE SPIRIT OF SHINTO IS THE SPIRIT OF NATURE

Shinto began as a "nature religion" thousands of years ago, and it has always been closely interwoven with nature's world. Growing things prove to the Shintoist that life has purpose within itself and helps you to understand the problem of inequality, suffering, pain and pleasure. Nature is the great teacher. Just as some trees bear the full force of the streaming sun, knowing that they were made to shelter and protect, so some people have such a role to play in life. And as there are other trees which seem destined to struggle in order to subsist, so also it is with certain people. It is all a matter of the *kami* working out their specific wish and will. There are trees which give only shade, and those which give both shade and fruit, each according to its nature. All life is interrelated with the *kami* and with every other life as well. For the *kami* are like men, and men are like trees, fulfilling, self-creating, expressing themselves. Such is the belief of Shinto (*Kami-No-Michi*), the Way of the Gods.

TORII—THE SYMBOL OF SHINTO

Near the entrance to the pathway leading to the shrine, you see the torii standing. This structure, consisting of two tall wooden uprights across which rests a straight or slightly curved crosspiece, is the emblem of Japan as well as the most famous symbol of Shinto. You remember how your father first pointed out a torii to you and explained how the huge pillars had once been massive trees which had given their lives so that they might serve the gods in a special way. Then he told you a Shinto story. "For a hundred years," he said, "the torii trees lived in the forest and then one day the woodsmen came with a white-robed priest. They went from one giant tree to another, judging each for height and size and for what the priest called 'uprightness.' Coming to the finest tree in the forest, the priest laid his hand on it and said, 'This is the chosen one.'

"Then the woodsmen counseled together on how and where it should fall and which other trees would have to be cleared to make way for its falling. Soon there was the sound of sawing and chopping which the priest said made a man think of his own passing. But neither the judgment of the ax nor the verdict of the saw nor the anguished crash of the chosen tree drowned the whisper moving through the forest, a whisper that said, 'When the sky is clear, and the wind hums in the fir trees, it is the heart of God revealing Himself.' "

The torii always took you back to the heart of nature. Even when the torii is painted red, as it often is, it has symbolism for you. Red is a sign of life, and the red coloring tells you that the torii trees still live. Even when men of other lands and other religions refer to Shinto as a primitive, animistic faith, rooted in superstition, it does not disturb you. Does not every religion see an attribute of God in the sun and sky, and behold His greatness in a mountain, and feel His presence in the trees?

WHATEVER IS, IS KAMI, AND KAMI IS GOD

There is, of course, a difference between Shinto and other faiths. In Shinto the attributes of things themselves are gods, whole and complete. Some religions call this pantheism, the doctrine that the universe itself is God. To you pantheism is not an offensive term, for you conceive the universe as *kami*. There are millions of *kami*, and the aggregate of these is God, although each *kami* is a god, too. *God is not a god seated on a throne. He is, as far as you are concerned, a co-ordinated creative substance.* And though there are meanings within meanings and unfoldment upon unfoldment, when you reach the heart of anything, the heart is *kami*. Dissect the seed from which the pine tree grows, you will not find *kami*, but *kami* is there. It is the seed's will-to-realize-itself. Give a rough stone to a sculptor and he will turn it into a thing of beauty; give an artist a crayon and a piece of paper and he will create an immortal scene; touch a poor, lonely person with love and he will be transformed into a happy individual. All is *kami*, and *kami* alone is truth.

So you pass beneath the torii and onward along the path; a wide, free path, meticulously clean, as is everything in and around a shrine. Huge stone lanterns which line your way are symbolical of the light of the *kami* guiding you. When you are in view of the shrine, which is actually a temple, a large, attractive structure built of wood and painted a soft red, you know you are approaching a holy place. You admire the gracefully sloping roofs and the customary *chigi,* crossed beams, sticking up at both ends of the gable boards and broad, inviting wooden steps are waiting to admit you to the quiet surroundings of this house of God. Nearby is the *shamusho,* a building provided for the priests as a place of special meditation. Here, too, are sacred trees, mostly the majestic cryptomeria, and many of them are encircled with a strand of rope called *shimenawa.* Colorful paper strips have been draped over the rope by worshipers as a sign of special gratitude to the gods.

THE WAY OF WORSHIP IS THE WAY OF THE GODS

You make your ablutions at a fountain in the shrine yard. By washing your hands and rinsing your mouth with clear, fresh water, you remind yourself that this purification symbolizes your desire to be clean in word and deed. Then you approach the temple as you would approach a beloved friend, for this house of the *kami* is, indeed, a living thing.

At the steps you pause to remove your shoes before entering the *haiden,* the spacious room for public worship. In front of you is the holy sanctuary with its cloth-covered altar. It is much like the household altar in your home before which you and your parents frequently worship. On it are a mirror—a symbol of the sun goddess—and a number of amulets or talismen, many of which have been brought here from other shrines where the same tutelary *kami* is worshiped. These wand-like talismen, called *gohei,* have jagged strips of paper protruding from their hollow tops. These are sacred, for it is believed that the spirits of the *kami* are particularly near the *gohei* and that their spirits may actually dwell in these tubes.

Fruit, rice and wine are also on the altar as offerings of respect to the activating *kami.* The *kami's* name, artistically written on rice paper or wood, is concealed behind a sacred curtain. You carry the same name as an amulet on your person to remind you at all times of the deep affinity you enjoy with your god.

Now you make your *hairei*, or invocation, by advancing to the altar where you bow twice deeply and solemnly. Then you clap your hands twice and bow in silent prayer. Sometimes you may also ring a small bell or sound a gong, not to "call the god," as many non-Shintoists believe, but to tender a gesture of respect as an announcement to yourself that God and you are here together. Your prayer will not be a request for help or a petition to a god with whom you can bargain; prayer, for you, is an act of remembrance. In such moments of reverence, you remind yourself that the divine spirit is your spirit. Yours is a natural religion, which means that by the very nature of life you are in harmony with the *kami*.

RELIGION IS A WAY OF REMEMBERING

Here, to this temple, your mother brought you thirty-two days after you were born to introduce you to the deity. The clean-shaven priest, wearing a white silk *ikan* (a full-sleeved clerical garment), wooden sandals and a *kanmuri*, a high-backed cap, blessed you in the name of the god whom your family worshiped. Then when you were five years old, your mother took you there again, on November 15, which is the day when children pray for protection during their growing-up period. This was your "confirmation" in the Shinto faith and with it began your frequent visits to various shrines where you learned that Shinto emphasizes cleanliness and beauty. You were taught that the *kami* delight in artistic, beautiful things, and you were shown how, even in the arrangement of flowers and in calligraphy, the spirit of the gods is revealed.

Later you came to the shrine to be married in a simple, impressive ceremony. Marriage, the priest explained, is arranged through the will and guidance of heaven. Shinto priests themselves are married and try to make their homes exemplary. Emphasizing the joy and blessedness which children bring to a home, the priest assured you that it is the *kami* that breathes life into a new-born child. He also reminded you that worship is a way of reinforcing your faith, and that in it you find the secret of true happiness. That is why Shinto temples stand open day and night for meditation and prayer.

The priest's counsel often returns to you as you stand with bowed head before the altar. Through silent contemplation you reflect on life and seek to come to terms with your *"kami-self."* Then you give thanks and conclude your period of meditation by pronouncing special words of blessing on your loved ones, your priest, yourself and others. Bowing twice in gratitude to the deity, you thank him for the privilege of worship and make an offering of money. This act is called *saimotsu* or *saisen*, and in many temples it is customary to toss the money through a grill into a submerged vault.

Shinto provides many instructions for spiritual improvement. There is, for example, the practice of *misogi*, intended to remove sin and pollution from the body and mind by the use of water, which is said to have originated with the god, Izanagi, who purified himself by bathing in sea water. The ceremony includes the use of special prayers, recited while standing near the sea, and splashing salt water over the body. Another ceremony, *saikai*, intended for anyone who wishes to go into deeper religious study, consists of remaining in seclusion for a certain period—from three days to seven days—while he devotes himself to fasting and prayer and continuous concentration on spiritual thoughts.

THE SHIFTING HISTORY OF SHINTO

But Shinto, like many ancient religions, is changing and had you been born a Shintoist, you would realize that during your lifetime the transition seems to have accelerated. You remember the cataclysmic years of the war, when Shinto nearly died. In the tragic aftermath, in defeat, your country was compelled to redefine its religious faith. For nearly 2000 years Shinto had been a state religion with taxes levied for the support of shrines, priests, and many extravagant festivals. *The high priest of Shinto was the emperor himself who, in a very real way, was a deity to be honored and worshiped.* Because emperor worship was rooted solidly in tradition and had come down to you along with your earliest religious and folk beliefs, you never questioned the emperor's motives or actions. Whenever he passed near you, you stood with eyes closed and head bowed in reverence.

The history of emperor worship, dating back to the eighth century, was authoritatively recorded in the ancient chronicles of your faith, in books called the *Kojiki* and the *Nihon Shoki*. They made it clear that the ancestors of the emperors were the gods themselves. They told of a god and a goddess named Izanagi and Izanami who stood on the bridge of heaven when the earth was being formed. Gazing down upon the aimless, drifting land, Izanagi seized a jeweled spear and stirred a portion of the formless earth. He churned the brine until it became a thing of beauty unlike anything the gods had seen. Then he drew out the spear and the sparkling creations of land that fell from it became the islands of Japan. The tallest point, formed when the tip of Izanagi's spear was lifted out, became sacred Fujiyama, the majestic volcanic mountain which rises more than twelve thousand feet into the sky. The first ruler of this earthly paradise was the son of the sun goddess, Amaterasu O-Mi-Kami, and his loyal subjects were the people who descended from Izanagi and Izanami.

The emperor was not only considered divine, but he was believed to rule as co-regent with the sun goddess at his side. She was symbolized by a sacred mirror which the emperor always kept beside him on his throne. He ruled by a decree more holy than that of the royalty of other nations and more compelling than the heads of other faiths. Who would ever have guessed that he could be shorn of his divinity?

But the years brought changes to your country. The attack on Pearl Harbor, precipitated by ambitious war lords, and the ensuing war wreaked suffering and defeat which all the Shinto *kami* could not withhold. *Under the treaty signed with the conqueror, the United States, the emperor was compelled to renounce his divinity.* When, on January 1, 1946, he disclaimed his godship, he became as much a mortal as his fellowmen. No longer were people compelled to address him as the "Divine Mikado" or "Son of the Most High" and, even though the mirror remained on his throne, the image of the sun goddess waned and threatened to disappear.

SHINTO OF THE STATE
AND SHINTO OF THE PEOPLE

Throughout the years of emperor worship, there had been only one officially recognized Shinto movement: State Shinto or *Kokka.* Governed by royal decree, it compelled the people to contribute to the upkeep of the Shinto shrines. It supported the priests. It trained the leaders and teachers of Shinto. It directed the festivals and holy days. It was a political, social and economic movement which loyal subjects had long suspected was being used to further governmental interests. There had been rumors that not only was the imperial family using Shinto for personal advantage, but that certain priests found it a source of personal prestige. Various schismatic Shinto sects and independent shrines made their appearance under the name of Sectarian Shinto or *Kyoha,* but it was not until the signing of the treaty at the end of World War II that freedom of religion came to Japan and that these non-State Shinto groups were recognized.

You had mingled feelings about this rapid turn of events. You wondered whether this might be the end of Shinto, for the Americans who occupied Japan made little attempt to understand Shinto's teachings or appreciate their meaning. But you also hoped that now, perhaps for the first time, your people could explore the deeper meaning of the faith, unhampered by restrictions of the past. Now, at last, Shinto would have to depend on its own merit and prove its worth. What did it have to offer? Could it justify its existence over the other religions of Japan, particularly Buddhism and Christianity? And somehow you felt that even though a treaty had deprived the emperor of his religious rule, he would ever continue to be a symbol of the *kami* and the Shinto faith.

Many State Shintoists seemed to agree. They predicted that as Japan once more prospered and gained in world prestige, its future emperors would again assume the role of deity-kings. Such predictions were only partially founded in fact. As Japan again began to grow in power and importance, it dreamed, to be sure, of its history and its myths, and many Shintoists continued to ask, "What if the emperor truly *is* divine? What if the sun-goddess *is* reflected in the sacred mirror? Will it not be necessary for the people to acknowledge this if it be true?" The major festivals, interrelated with the life of the country, also continued as an assurance that the partnership between Shinto and nationalism had never been dissolved in the minds of many people. Behind the mortality of the imperial family still looms the glory of the immortal gods, and devout State Shintoists never forget that the word for government and festival in the Japanese language is one and the same: *matsuri-goto,* or that the Land of the Rising Sun is still the land of the *kami* and that the *kami* are still the keepers of Japan.

But had you been born a Shintoist, you would realize that, though State Shinto continues to be important, the Shinto of the people, called Sectarian Shinto, is growing ever more important. It consists of thirteen groups, which developed strongly, though often unobtrusively, during the past century. These had support of great masses of people who had grown restless under the formalism of State Shinto. *Sectarian Shinto became the religion of the Japanese "reformation." It was destined to come despite war or treaties, but the de-deification of the emperor hastened its recognition as a movement of major importance in Japanese life.* Sectarian Shinto now has its own independent organizations, headquarters, shrines and priests. It is geared to the people's needs. It combines spiritual healing with the tradition of old Shinto, positive thinking with the creative power of the ancient *kami,* and a new, modern interpretation of nature and nature's God.

THE SHINTO REFORMATION

Had you been born a Shintoist, you could not escape the impact of these groups which make up this modern Shinto "revival" movement. You would be impressed with their vitality and growth, their leaders, their missionary zeal, their boldness, and their vision for the future. There is, for example, the movement called Tenrikyo, whose foundress, Miki Nakayama, believed that the great *Kami,* whom she identifies as "God the Parent," called her to be his "living temple." After this revelation she set out to help other people find "the good life" and true happiness by clearing their minds of the "dust of imperfection." Today Tenrikyo is designed to rid humanity of this "dust" through many dramatic rituals.

You would have heard of Konko-kyo, the religion which teaches that the universe is the Grand Shrine of the Parent-God, that there is no devil and no hell, and that the love of God is in and around every individual. You would know about Kurozumi-Kyo, named after its founder, Kurozumi Munetada. It affirms that Amaterasu-O-Mi-Kami is the creator of all things, and that every soul is in harmony with the divine source of light and life.

There are many others which, though they would not profess to be "pure Shinto," nonetheless, have great Shinto influence combined with a syncretism representative of other faiths and personal revelations. Such groups are the famous and highly prominent Omoto, also Fusokyo, Izumo Taishakyo, Shinrikyo, Shinshukyo, Mitakekyo, Shinto Taikyo, Shinto Taiseikyo, Jikkokyo, Misogikyo and Shinto Shuseiha. These and other movements are challenging your people and continue to express the deep spiritual quest of the people of Japan.

FAITH MEANS FESTIVALS

Surrounded by so many new sects and confronted by a shrine in every *caza-mura* (the smallest subdivision of local government), you would feel yourself a part of a vital and meaningful faith. The Shinto year is dotted with festivals even as the land is marked by toriis. Most of these are village festivals which means that all of the people, even those who do not embrace Shinto, participate. In ancient days there were customarily four work days in succession followed by a fifth day designated as a day of rest sacred to a deity. The rest day was usually a festival day; the largest and most important one occurring at planting time and at the time of harvest.

Among the many spectacular festival days are such occasions as *Ennichi,* the "deity's day," on which your people go to the shrines en masse. It is believed that special guidance can be gained if this day is rightly observed. Because of the large crowds of worshipers, vendors are on hand and booths are set up to sell fruits and flowers and incense which may be offered to the gods.

Other significant festivals are *On-Bashira-Sal*, a ceremony of tree planting which takes place every seven years in the four corners of the shrine or temple grounds; the *Naoi Ceremony* is designed to help rid oneself of bad luck. In this the participants jostle one another in an attempt to touch the scapegoat and thereby rub off their bad luck on him. *Jidai* festival, in which worshipers, dressed in costumes of a thousand years ago, bless the city of Kyoto, the ancient capital of Japan. There are also fire ceremonies which honor the fire *kami,* and cherry blossom festivals to praise the gods of beauty and the spring. There are *matsuris* (festivals) to praise the gods of the sea, the mountains, the villages and most important of all, the gods of the rice fields who help provide the "staff of life" for your people.

There are also special days when portable shrines or *mi-koshi* are used. These elaborate "floats" commemorate occasions when, it was believed, the ancient deities traveled from one temple to another. On the day of the *Minato* festival, the portable shrine is carried around Matsushima Bay in a boat to remind people that the gods also sanctified the water as well as the land. Another festival, the *Otariya,* is celebrated by parading small shrines through village streets as a ritual against the outbreak of fires. There are many other *matsuri* contrived to control floods, to avert typhoons, to protect against political unrest, to honor the dead, and to celebrate all sorts of historical events.

Few non-Shintoists realize the importance of the *matsuri*. They do not know that many peasants would not begin their cultivation in the early spring without a festival, nor would they harvest their crops without a ritual in which the first fruits are dedicated to the *kami*. The palanquins of the deities are important and prized possessions in almost every village and the Shinto liturgical year is spun on the *matsuri*, a word which actually means that one should lift up his heart to the gods.

Devout Shintoists would not embark on a trip or board a plane or a ship without first going to a temple-shrine. All of the Shinto people are sentimental about their religion, but they are not fanatical, as some non-Shintoists believe them to be.

SHINTO AND THE KAMIKAZE

People who do not understand your faith often associate Shinto with many bizarre concepts. They believe, for example, that Shintoism was responsible for the conduct of airplane pilots who, during the war, resorted to suicidal bombings. You have often heard it said that these pilots, called *kamikaze,* were obeying Shinto laws. While some of these men may have been Shintoists, their acts were not Shinto-inspired. They were, rather, the result of an ancient nationalistic tradition which embodied the belief that it was honorable to die for the fatherland. The *kamikaze* were the modern version of the ancient *samurai,* those feudal warriors of fierce and fearless skill who carried two swords as emblems of their profession. The *samurai* adhered to a code, called *bushido,* which put valor and courage above life, and out of which grew a legend that those who died according to *bushido* received special blessings in the life to come. Out of *bushido* came the practice of *hara-kiri,* death by falling on one's own sword. But *bushido* also emphasized many good principles, such as purity in body, diligence in thought, and fidelity in action. But the things foreigners remembered most were sensational acts like *hara-kiri* and *kamikaze.*

You regret that people do not understand your faith, but you realize it is also difficult for you to understand the religions of other countries. You cannot grasp the meaning of "evangelism" or "missionary" activity in other faiths. It is quite impossible for you to appreciate religions which are highly institutionalized and exclusive, for Shinto is a liberal and all-inclusive faith. Because everything in Shinto is spirit, how, then, is it possible to have religious divisions and sects or how can one religion be higher or lower than another?

Of course, Shinto *does* have its sects and its divisions, but you believe that these are merely external differences, rising out of the personality and beliefs of the founders and the inability of minds to grasp the total truth. As far as you are concerned, there is no rivalry in Shinto, no attempt to convert anyone, no effort to lure anyone away from any other faith. *All Shintoists believe that the essence of God is the essence of life and that the essence of life is the eternal substance of every individual. God is good; man is good; man, therefore, is God.* How, then, can there be any quarrel about basic principles?

SHINTO AND BUDDHISM

You believe that a person can be a Christian or a Jew or a Moslem or a Buddhist and still be a good Shintoist because of the universality of the divine spirit. In fact, many good Shintoists *are* good Buddhists. There was a time in the eighteenth and nineteenth centuries when people predicted that Buddhism would absorb Shinto, but they did not know how deeply Shinto had penetrated the Japanese mind. How could an imported religion like Buddhism, which reached Japan both from China and Korea in the sixteenth century, ever unseat the *kami?* Buddhism was pessimistic; Shinto was optimistic. Buddhism talked about Nirvana and future bliss; Shinto emphasized the now and present bliss. Buddhism was intellectual; Shinto was inspirational. Buddhism taught asceticism, subjugation of life, a philosophy of triumph over suffering; Shinto taught the fulness of life "unphilosophically," by urging an intuitive grasp of the presence of God in the universe and in a man's own heart. But Buddhism and Shinto also have much in common, so have Confucianism and Shinto. All believe in spiritual universality; all have an affection for the genial temperament of Japan; and all have a deep respect for ancestor worship.

HONOR THE DEAD AND YOU
HONOR THE LIVING

You do not expect everyone to understand your veneration for your ancestors because not everyone understands the Shinto concept which contends that every person is a divine spirit individualized. If this fact of personified divinity is true, then it follows that every man may also be a god; and if you wish to revere your departed loved ones as gods, you feel it is your privilege and, in a way, your duty to do so. Although your departed loved ones may be a bit lower than the great *kami* in spiritual perfection, they are, nonetheless, worthy of a shrine and deserving of devotion.

Near your home or in a sacred place in a grove, near a lake, or close to a shrine, you have your *tamaya*, a memorial altar enshrining the spirits of the dead. You put a mirror in the shrine on the back of which the ancestral names are etched, or you inscribe their names on a scroll. You often go to the shrine for meditation and let your mind dwell on the heritage left you by your loved ones. You are in their line of ascent to an ever-evolving noble life. Frequently you place a twig of a sacred tree on the shrine or leave a *tamagushi*, a strip of paper which bears a greeting or a prayer.

Had you been born a Shintoist, you would have no fear of death, for death is a part of life and cannot be avoided, bypassed, or escaped. Life is self-creative because the *kami* is in every individual, and the *kami* never dies. So whether you are buried or cremated, whether your funeral is conducted by a Shinto priest, a Buddhist, or a Confucianist, you believe that your spirit is immortal.

In Shinto, heaven is a "high-up, sacred world," the dwelling place of the most superior *kami*. *Ame-tsuchi* is a word which has great meaning for you, for *Ame* is heaven and *tsuchi* is earth. A Shinto myth explains that, at the time of creation, the purest and most brilliant elements, more brilliant even than the beauty of Japan, branched off to become *ame*, while the other elements branched off to become *tsuchi*. Consequently, *ame* is where the sacred deities make their home; *tsuchi* is where the gods live when they come to earth. It is never quite clear to you whether all gods are incarnated as human beings, nor is "heaven" entirely clear to you, but you are confident that the *kami* within you has a destiny which is good and that some day *ame* will be yours to experience.

So you continue your worship, and as a devoted Shintoist you perform your worship at your household altar or god-shelf every morning and every night. Each time you take with you a small bowl of rice, a cup of *sake* (rice whisky), and a bit of fruit as an offering of respect and loyalty. You place a twig of *sakaki* or a flower in a vase and light some incense or a lamp. You remain there in silent meditation while you worship the *kami*. Sometimes you journey to a major shrine (*jinja*) like Meiji or Izumo or Ise where you can attend dramatic ceremonies and watch the elaborately costumed temple dancers enact intricate rituals to the accompaniment of fifes and drums. Or you witness the famous *No* plays which are narrative and operatic dramas portraying some phase of Shinto life.

The beauty of these presentations, the inspiration of the priests, the propitiatory offering, and the prayers persuade you to live an even better life. Shinto has no commandments, no rules for conduct. Nor does it have a saviour or a messiah or someone comparable to Jesus, Buddha, or Mohammed. It has no scriptures and no sutras and, actually, no thrilling history to relate. Its holy book is the universe; its creed the good life; its gods the *kami*. These are enough to unite earth and heaven and to remind you of the symbolical torii upon which Izanagi and Izanami stood when first the world was made. They looked down on the lovely islands of Japan and called them good. And so would you, had you been born a Shintoist.

6

Had You Been Born

a Jew

HAD YOU BEEN BORN A JEW, your greatest heritage would be
the spiritual history of your people. It is a heritage recorded
in the Torah, the Hebrew scriptures; preserved in the Talmud
and Midrash, which are rabbinical writings and commentaries
on the law; and channeled through the lives of ancient prophets
and modern scholars—a heritage as old as Canaan and as new as
the state of Israel. It is linked together by holy days unerringly
kept throughout the tides of time. It is epitomized in the centuries
of captivity and persecution; it is the victory of a people. But, most
of all, it is represented in a way of life challengingly designed
for 12,000,000 Jews throughout the modern world.

YOUR RELIGION AND YOU

The interplay between the history of your religion and the
history of every individual Jew is also part of your heritage. You
cannot separate your destiny from that of Judaism. Whatever
affects your religion affects you, and whatever happens to you

leaves its influence upon the nature of your faith. In no other religion is this relationship between faith's profession and faith's practice so clearly defined, or the connection between God and man so intimate. The long march of Judaism from the earliest recorded event to the present moment is relived by every Jew. Your life is the spiritual history of Israel personified.

When Moses, the spokesman for God, said, "Hear, O Israel, the Lord our God, the Lord is One," it was an event in history, but it was also a specific event in your life. The first prayer you learned, the first religious thought impressed upon your mind consisted of these very words, "Hear, O Israel, the Lord our God, the Lord is One." This declaration of faith marked the beginning of your personal spiritual pilgrimage, just as it did the age-old pilgrimage of your people. Before you, too, lay a world unknown and uncharted. You were instructed to recall the words every morning and night, to remember them in sickness and in health, and to breathe them at the hour of death, just as your fore-fathers had done in the days when Judaism was young, when, throughout the vicissitudes of their nomadic roamings they prayed, "Hear, O Israel, the Lord our God, the Lord is One."

When these words were first spoken, Mount Sinai was the axis of monotheism. The God of Moses bore distinctive features which the gods of other religions had never portrayed; the gods of ancient civilizations had many names and many faces; their genealogies were fictionized with legends and myths. The God of Moses stood authoritatively alone. There were no other gods before Him; there were to be no other gods after Him. He was the beginning and the end; not a god motivated by human beings or molded into an image by the priest-craft, but the living Creator of all things, the Judge of all men, the Lord of all the world.

I AM THAT I AM!

Who was this God? Where was His habitation and what was His name? You often asked these questions, just as they were asked by Moses who lived some 3500 years ago.

One day Moses said to the Lord, "When I come unto the chil-dren of Israel and say, 'The God of your fathers hath sent me unto you'; and they shall say to me, 'What is His name?' what shall I say unto them?"

And God said, "I Am That I Am! Thus shalt thou say unto the children of Israel, 'I Am hath sent me unto you.'"

Early in your life you learned, as did the Israelites, that God is the great I AM, with a name so sacred it was never spoken. When it was first written, it was YHWH, an unpronounceable term of reverence; then He was called Elohim and Adonay, even as He is today.

Your understanding of this God was deepened when you began your studies of the Torah, which means the beginning of wisdom and the knowledge of the love of God. *Torah, which means divine instruction, embraces the whole broad field of religious study, but the Torah is specifically a sacred parchment scroll containing the Pentateuch or the Law of Moses.* It is Judaism's most revered devotional object, so sacred, in fact, that when it is worn out it is reverently buried in a grave. Men who copy the Torah, those who make these holy scrolls, are called Sofers (scribes) and seek to lead especially exemplary lives. The Torah resides in the ark in every synagogue, the Jewish place of worship. Synagogue, which means a bringing together of the people, was soon used to designate the place where the people met.

The ark in the synagogue is sacrosanct. In the wilderness wanderings of the early Israelites, the sacred ark, considered to be the dwelling place of Yahweh, was an oblong chest of acacia wood overlaid with gold. Called the "ark of the covenant," because it contained the stones upon which the Ten Commandments were written, it also bore the "mercy seat," a golden plate surrounded by cherubs, upon which the blood of sacrificial animals was sprinkled. Because the ark also represented the abiding presence of the Lord, a replica of the ark is found in every synagogue today, usually in the eastern wall. Perpetually burning before it is a votive light, a symbol of the light of God illuminating His children's way. It is a constant reminder to you, as well as to Israel, that you are in His presence and care.

At every Sabbath service, while the worshipers respectfully stand, the rabbi, who is the spiritual teacher, solemnly takes the

Torah from the ark, unrolls it, and reads a portion of the familiar words:

> "I am the Lord thy God who brought thee out of the land of Egypt, out of the house of bondage.
>
> Thou shalt have no other gods before me.
>
> Thou shalt not make unto thee any graven image, or any likeness of any thing that is in heaven above, or that is in the earth beneath, or that is in the water under the earth. . . ." (Exodus 20; 2-4)

Thoughtfully listening, you realize what a profound influence the Ten Commandments have had upon the world, how they have become the basis for civil laws; how they have been made the cardinal tenets of other great religions; and how they have been taught to many people. To no one, however, are they more meaningful than to the Jew, for the history of Judaism is his history. Always there is the inseparable link between this history, the people of Israel, and you.

BAR MITZVAH

When you began your study of the Torah, your teacher placed a drop of honey on the page to symbolize the joy and sweetness of religious wisdom. Through its thousands of years of history, Judaism refined what it found in other religions and created the greatest literary treasure of all time. Written almost exclusively in Hebrew, the Torah of the Law, the Nebiim or the Prophets, and the Kethubim or Sacred Writings (called by Christians the Hagiographa) are the official documents of your religion and the basis of faith and morals for Israel and you.

When you were twelve, you were introduced to these sacred writings in the ceremony of Bar Mitzvah, and as a male child of the Jewish faith, you sensed the deep significance of the occasion. Bar Mitzvah means "son of duty" and the ceremony, a solemn and auspicious event, marks the end of childhood and the coming of age in spiritual responsibility. In liberal Judaism, such as the Reform and Conservative movements, girls also share the rite of Bar Mitzvah.

In this period of study, out of which grew the Christian practice of catechetical instruction and confirmation, you were reminded how the individual life is related to the spiritual life of your people. The solemnization of the ceremony was heightened by your participation in the public reading of the Torah in the Hebrew language. Your parents, to honor you on this important day, made it a special event by inviting your relatives and the rabbi to a memorable dinner. It was a day of great happiness for you and for your elders, who recalled the time they made their Bar Mitzvah and how the meaning of it had increased for them throughout the years. They explained that often when controversies arose as to how a deed should be done or how a decision should be made, the rabbi was questioned, "What does the Mitzvah dictate?" Because the doctrine of Mitzvah is a frame of reference for life and conduct, it becomes the touchstone by which duties are imposed in accordance with its teaching.

Judaism is so rich in tradition that every religious act has its roots far back in history. For example, among the gifts you received at Bar Mitzvah was a lovely mezuzah, meaning "doorpost," which is a little box or tube containing verses from the Torah. It is often placed outside the door of Jewish homes to show that the family is loyal to the faith and the teaching of Judaism. Mezuzahs, much like the phylacteries which priests of old wore on the forehead or on the left arm, are still worn by traditional Jews who believe that God commanded such action for all time when He said, "It shall be for a sign upon thee, upon thine hand, and for a memorial between thine eyes, that the Lord's law may be in thy mouth." (Exodus 13:8,9)

THE LAW AND LOVE OF GOD

The Lord's law and the Lord's love seem to you to describe best the ancient mooring of your faith and to assure you that God is both just and merciful. The Prophet Isaiah said, "He is our Father, our Redeemer for everlasting." Over and over the sacred scriptures make clear that the God of Israel is a just God because He loves righteousness, and a jealous God because He loves His people with paternal compassion. This concept of the Fatherhood of God, immortalized through the history of Judaism, is at the very center of your personal faith.

The scribes and scholars of Judaism have probed into every line and letter of God's holy word. In no other religion have men mined so deeply and so earnestly into the secret depths of truth. There are books which only the adepts understand, books like the Zohar, a mystical study of the innermost nature of God and man; books relating to the cabala or hidden doctrines; books from the pre-exilic and post-exilic periods with the Babylonian captivity forming the break between the two; books with prophetic writings, prayers, poems, proverbs; and books which are part of the brilliant literature of the Moorish supremacy in Spain. But when all is said and done, the heart of Judaism comes back to God's love and God's law which comprise the divine teaching.

The details of the teaching of Yahweh were handed down by oral tradition until the end of the second century A.D. when, after having been systematically defined by rabbinical councils, they were incorporated in the Mishnah or writings of instruction. The Mishnah, which formed the basis for the Talmud, is the name for Judaism's civil and canonical rules of conduct. The text of the Talmud is called the Mishnah and the commentary is the Gemara.

MEN AND MOVEMENTS

The immortal figures in the history of your faith are as familiar to you as the members of your own household. Abraham, first of the patriarchs and father of the Hebrews, seems not to be legendary, but real; a man who walked with the God whom Moses was later to reveal. His son, also a very real personage of flesh and blood, was Isaac who, as the husband of Rebekah and the father of Jacob and Esau, propounded significant truths and parables. It was Jacob, called Israel, who was the progenitor of your faith, for it is through his twelve sons that the history of your religion unfolds. Moses, the prophets, the men and women of Biblical history were people of destiny.

So were men like the Maccabees who, during the second century B.C., freed your people from the yoke of Syrian oppression; Hillel the Elder, (B.C. 30-9 A.D.) a sage of Judaism who told his followers, "What is hateful to thee, do not unto thy fellowman; this is the whole Law. The rest is but commentary." There were also men like Philo Judaeus (30 B.C.-50 A.D.) who is known as the Plato of Judaism; doctors of the law like Shammai and Gamaliel; Spanish-born Moses Maimonides (1135-1204), a pre-eminent philosopher; Polish-born Haym Salomon, patriot of the American Revolution; German-born Moses Mendelsohn, scholar and humanist; American-born Abraham Mordecai, famous pioneer; and many more. But when the philosophy of these men is winnowed, it is found to be the expression of God's will embodied in the holy teachings.

This is also true of the groups within Judaism. From Hasidism, a pietistical movement of the eighteenth century, to Reconstructionism, a modern attempt to discover how man can best come to terms with life and his times, Judaism is a religion of many types with three major groups serving the majority of modern Jews in their spiritual needs: the Orthodox, the Conservative and the Reform, each of which claims well over a million members in the United States.

Orthodox Judaism is the continuation of ancient authority with all its traditional social, religious and dietary customs. Reform Judaism is the liberal or progressive movement which has sought to adjust itself to the shifting times without losing what it believes to be the basic spiritual, ethical and ceremonial aspects of the faith. Conservative Judaism is the middle-of-the-road Judaic expression, recognizing the authority of ritual Law and the need for preserving the unique characteristics of Judaism in the modern world.

Zionism, a movement attempting to return the Jew to Palestine, cuts across these "denominational" lines. That God wanted His people to have a homeland is believed by most Jews as well as by many gentiles who believe this to be a divine prophecy. Ever since their exile and the capture and destruction of their land by the Romans in A.D. 70, the Jews have longed to return to Jerusalem. This hope was continually incorporated in the prayers and dreams of the Jewish people, who considered such a restoration the fulfillment of a prophecy.

In this connection, early Zionism was strongly apocalyptic. Modern Zionism, as interpreted by Theodor Herzl of Vienna, was based upon the need for a homeland, a state which Judaism could call its own and where Jews could live together in harmony, adhering to their respective traditions. Another interpreter, Asher Ginsberg, insisted that the homeland should be more than a political or cultural habitat; it should above all represent a spiritual haven where the faith, customs and language of a people would be perpetuated. In every instance, the idea of Zion was always closely allied with the country which the Prophet Zechariah had designated as the "Holy Land." (Zechariah 2:13).

Finally, after nearly twenty centuries of homelessness and wandering, centuries filled with captivity, exile, ghettos and attempts by anti-semites to totally annihilate the people and the religion that make up Judaism, the Jewish people began to see the culmination of their hopes and dreams. After having been dispersed across the world, having become citizens of almost every nation, yet rarely fully accepted in any country, Jews learned that the Zionist movement, vigorously led by Dr. Chaim Weizmann since 1917, had triumphed. The United Nations General Assembly voted on November 29, 1947, to partition Palestine into two independent states: Jewish Israel and Arab Jordan. On May 14, 1948, the proclamation was sealed. For Judaism it was the fifth day of the month of Iyar in the 5708 year of its history. In Palestine, where God had first revealed Himself, a group of modern Jewish pioneers, statesmen and religionists, came to mark-off the prescribed boundaries of their habitation. David Ben-Gurion, first prime minister of the new state, read the Jewish Declaration of Independence. This was followed by the Jewish National Anthem, the *Hatikvah*, which means "The Hope." Prayers were spoken. The land was blessed. Israel was established.

It was a small, almost captive country. On its west stretched the broad expanse of the Mediterranean, on the north lay Lebanon and Syria, on the south loomed Egypt, and on the east was Jordan. Designated as its capital was Jerusalem, the holy city, but as it was a disputed territory, sacred to Arab and Jew alike, only a portion belonged to the immigrants. Israel, which called its section the "New City," was confronted across a neutral corridor by the "Old City" ruled by Jordan. The United Nations, adopting a resolution to internationalize Jerusalem, was unable to get support from either Israel or Jordan. So the historic city remained divided, the uneasy homeland for both nations; a city mutually shared, but jealously cherished and guarded by each.

The state of Israel, with less than 10,000 square miles of land and a population of some 2,000,000 was prepared from the very start to provide a habitat for all those who revered the Star of David, the emblem which is emblazoned on its flag. With typical Jewish tenacity, its citizens have transformed the hills and valleys. With characteristic foresight, spurred by traditional love for learning, they have established outstanding schools, colleges and universities. Demonstrating their truly democratic nature, they have proclaimed freedom of religion to Jew and gentile alike.

JUDAISM AND OTHER FAITHS

Had you been born a Jew, you would often feel as though you were standing in the center of a whirling world of faith. Around you, other great religions are ambitiously evangelizing, proselytizing and zealously exhorting men in their specific ways of salvation. They have adopted many of your customs and concepts: the thirty-nine books which comprise your sacred scriptures are the "Old Testament" of Christendom; the Apocrypha, which Catholicism and certain Protestant groups have accepted, came from the Maccabean era. The old synagogues of Israel have also served as patterns for Christianity both in architectural design and in their order of worship. Even as it has been traditional that the synagogue should face the east and be built on the highest location so that it should dominate all other buildings in dignity and prominence, many Christian churches have been designed in like fashion.

And the ritualistic rites of your people have infiltrated into the Christian church. The Jew, before entering the synagogue, purifies his hands; upon entering, he touches his lips to the scriptures which are set near the entrance for this purpose. The reading of scripture lessons, the psalmody, the sermon, antiphonal singing, the giving of alms, the concept of confession—all have been incorporated into the Christian service. It has been said that the form of the Ante-Mass was taken over from the synagogue ritual, both in its structure and general function.

The Islamic people also borrowed heavily from your traditions and beliefs as reflected in the Koran, as seen in their monotheism, their veneration of prophets, their recognition of the Pentateuch and the Psalms, their ablutions, their facing toward Mecca—as your people faced toward Jerusalem during prayer—and in their dietary regulations. Circumcision is also practiced by the Islamic people, although not as a religious rite as it is among your people. In Judaism, it is a commandment (Genesis 17:10-14) signifying a covenant between God and Israel. It is an interesting fact that circumcision is commemorated in a holy day (the Circumcision of Jesus) in Catholic and Anglican churches even today. This "Feast of the Circumcision" is held on January first and confirms, for Christians, Jesus' respect for Jewish teaching in that He underwent the ceremony eight days after his birth.

There are divergent views among your people concerning this man Jesus whom Christians call the Christ. The name, Jesus, relating to the name Joshua and Isaiah and stemming from the same root, was common among the Hebrew people. Your historians, with the exception of Josephus, make no mention of any special "Jesus" as being important in the history of religion. Josephus, who flourished during the first century of the Christian era, simply mentions that a certain Jesus took up the preaching and gospel of John the Baptist following John's imprisonment by Herod Antipas who was tetrarch of Galilee between 4 and 40 A.D.

The hope of a promised messiah, around which so many religions are built, was and still is the hope of you and your people. The Israelites believed that when he came he would restore their nation in a special way, perhaps in a militant way, conquering their Roman oppressors. Jesus was acclaimed by some, but He did not consummate, for the great majority, the true messianic anticipation or fulfill what was believed should be the phophetic nature of his coming. Nor has any other prophet met the standards of this high calling. To this day, Judaism still awaits the Promised One of whom Isaiah said, "Behold my servant, who I uphold; mine elect in whom my soul delighteth; I have put my spirit upon him; he shall make the right to go forth to the nations. He shall not cry, nor lift up, nor cause his voice to be heard in the street. A bruised reed shall he not break, and the smoking flax shall he not quench; he shall bring forth judgment unto truth. He shall not fail nor be discouraged, till he have set right in the earth; and the isles shall wait for his teaching." (Isaiah 42:1-4)

You recognize the fact that some religions truly believe that Jesus was this Messiah. You are aware of the good these religions have achieved and you feel they all have something to offer, for there are as many religious views in the world as there are cultures and people. You have seen new religions expand and grow and have observed how, through the years, they have given evidence of change. You have seen Christianity in many of its areas of expression become more understanding of Judaism, but you have also seen evidences of intolerance and anti-semitism among many well-meaning people because of deep-seated misinformation and lack of information about your faith.

Many times your people have been made the object of prose-lytization and have been sought for "conversion" by various faiths. So deep-seated is Jewish teaching, that many Jews who became Christians in the days of the early Christian church sought to impose *their* rites and practices, such as dietary injunctions, fast-ing and circumcision upon their converters! These Jews were called "Judaizers."

Unlike Christianity or other mission-minded religions, modern Judaism has no desire to proselytize or persuade non-Jews to its point of view. As a Jew you are more concerned that the divine powers in man should be unfolded than that your religion should grow quantitatively. You feel that God-realization is the aim of humanity. You are convinced that the world is inherently good, and that evil is a figment of the mind of man, not a creation of the mind of God.

God is not a capricious monarch who controls human beings like a puppeteer does his dancing figures; God is a gracious Father who has generously endowed His children with freedom of choice. You believe that man was created good, that he came into the world free from sin, and that he brings with him the image and likeness of his Creator. As man is born of a benevolent God, so he may rest assured that when he dies he will also attain everlasting life. Immortality is in the nature of all men because it is in the nature of God.

Although Judaism is not an evangelistic movement, there are occasional conversions to your religion. By example and precept, rather than by preaching and persuasion, Judaism influences others. By stimulating intellectual pursuits and suggesting an ethical approach to contemporary problems, it seems peculiarly designed for the modern day, even though it is centuries old. Judaism is a way of life for people who believe they have a special service to perform, namely, to testify to the presence of God in the continuing history of the world. It seems to you that this should be the spirit of all true religions, and that it was most perfectly stated by one of your prophets when he said,

"He had shewed thee, O man, what is good; and what doth the Lord require of thee, but to do justly, and to love mercy, and to walk humbly with thy God." (Micah 6:8)

JUDAISM AND THE FAMILY

Idealistically, you are urged to walk and work with God in your daily vocation. In your home you endeavor to live as though God were the unseen Guest. Your home, fully as much as the synagogue, is a place of worship. Here the mother lights the Sabbath candles for the Friday evening meal and prayer. Here the father intones the ancient Hebrew Kiddush, "Blessed art Thou, O Lord, King of the Universe, who created the fruit of the vine." Here the children and parents observe the holy days and festivals. In no religion are there closer family ties than in Judaism. It may be that this is why there is so little delinquency among Jewish youth and so much maturity of thought among young people of the Jewish faith.

As your family is united by the observances of various holy days, so Jewish people around the world are united by the traditional festivals of Judaism's liturgical year. These days, designated by the Jewish calendar, were once strange and anachronistic to the gentile world, but gradually their significance and their interrelation with both Christian and seasonal holidays have become increasingly clear.

There is, for example, Rosh Hashana, the Jewish New Year, a moveable date occurring in September which, in your 12-month calendar, is the month of Tishri, Judaism's historic years are reckoned from 3761 B.C., and since the very beginning of its observance, Rosh Hashana has been a day of thoughtful soul-searching and rededication of life.

Yom Kippur, the Day of Atonement, occurring ten days after Rosh Hashana, is a period of solemn rest. This day, called a Sabbath of Sabbaths, is set aside for confession of sins, repentance and reconciliation with God. The Sabbath itself, which begins at dusk each Friday, although hallowed by all your people, is most rigorously observed by Orthodox Jews. Orthodoxy clearly states its commandments for the observance of this day: there shall be no working, no fighting, no traveling. The rites for Yom Kippur are prescribed in Leviticus 16 and the authority according to that Scripture is binding forever when it says, "For on that day shall the priest make an atonement for you, to cleanse you, that ye may be clean from all your sins before the Lord. It shall be a sabbath of rest unto you, and ye shall afflict your souls, by a statute forever."

There are other days which the faithful Jew will observe: Hanukkah, the Feast of Dedication, celebrated for eight days in late November or early December, honors the Maccabean victory over the Greeks who had sought to Grecianize the Jews in the second century B.C.; Purim, the festival of deliverance based on the story recorded in the Book of Esther and observed in February or March according to the lunisolar calendar of Judaism; Shabuoth, the Feast of Weeks, or feast of the first fruits of the harvest, also called Pentecost, which means "fifty days" after Passover; and Sukkoth, Feast of the Tabernacles or Booths, which commemorates the ingathering of the harvest.

But of all festivals none is more meaningful than Passover. Taking its name from *pazah* (to pass or skip over), it memorializes the tradition that the "angel of death" passed over those houses of the Israelites in Egypt which had been marked with the blood of the paschal lamb. It was this divine seal which spared the first-born in each house from being slain. This momentous event, recorded in Exodus 12, is a testimony that proclaims for you the faith of an individual and the faith of a collective people; it proclaims God's concern for every member of His family and His protection for His people as a race.

The majestic words that instituted the Passover are etched in your memory: "Then Moses called for all the elders of Israel, and said unto them, Draw out and take you a lamb according to your families, and kill the passover. And ye shall take a bunch of hyssop, and dip it in the blood that is in the basin, and strike the lintel and the two side posts with the blood that is in the basin; and none of you shall go out at the door of his house until the morning. For the Lord will pass through to smite the Egyptians; and when he seeth the blood upon the lintel, and on the two side posts, the Lord will pass over the door, and will not suffer the destroyer to come unto your houses to smite you. And ye shall observe this thing for an ordinance to thee and to thy sons for ever." (Exodus 12:21,24)

Christians, too, understand Passover; they observe it according to their own tradition, having made Jesus their "paschal lamb." Early Jewish Christians celebrated their belief in the death and resurrection of Jesus at Passover time. To this day the Jewish Passover and the Christian Easter share practically the same period, and the Passover tradition of your people has been preserved in the Christian celebration of their "Holy Week."

Passover, the holy time of *Pesach*, is a time when families gather in all Jewish homes; it is a sacred time when every Jew wishes to be at home with his people. Here on the first night (or the first and second nights), you gather for the significant and ever impressive seder service in which the suffering and deliverance of the Jews in Egypt are tenderly dramatized. Every Jewish child loves, honors and respects the seder. He knows its meaning. He is versed in the Haggadah, which is the text for this memorial and festive meal. No Jew ever forgets how he sat with his parents around the seder table and how, in the spell of tradition, he asked, "Why is this night different from all other nights?" And he recalls how his father answered, "We were slaves unto Pharaoh in Egypt, and the Eternal our God led us from there with a mighty hand."

You find deep within each festival the insistent reminder that Judaism has endured much, has been delivered often, and has been consistently saved from dissemination and absorption by the providence of God. And when you remember this, you realize that even as this is true for Judaism, it is true for you.

BASIC CONCEPTS OF JUDAISM

Had you been a born a Jew, you would realize that despite various types of Judaism and many speculations about Judaism by scholars and interpreters, there are certain beliefs that can be said to be fundamental to the nature of your faith. One statement of these beliefs was suggested by the scholar Hasdai Crescas, who, in the fifteenth century, listed fourteen points by which Judaism might better comprehend itself and through which others might better apprehend your faith:

1. God knows individually all things and all people.

2. His providence is over each individual.

3. He is omnipotent.

4. He revealed himself in a special way to the prophets.

5. He has given man freedom of the will.

6. He gave man the Torah.

7. He created the universe at a particular time.

8. Immortality is assured for those who observe his commandments.

9. There is punishment for the wicked.

10. The dead will be resurrected.

11. The Torah is eternal.

12. Moses is supreme.

13. The priest can foretell future events through the Urim and Thummim (objects mentioned in Exodus 28:30)

14. The Messiah will come.

These concepts are impressed upon you through the eternal beauty of the scripture. Your hear them everywhere in the teaching and in the interpretation of God's love and law. The rabbi speaks of them; the cantor, who sings the liturgical music in the synagogue, proclaims them; the festivals perpetuate them; and when the Promised One appears, He will eternalize them.

And so, as you review the history of Judaism as a religion, as a people, and as a nation, you are observing yourself in your own religious experiences. The qualities which made that history significant are those you need to comprehend in order to understand your destiny. Your fathers clung to their faith with marvelous tenacity and retained their racial characteristics with remarkable purity in the midst of alien peoples. Scattered among the nations of the world, they never admitted defeat nor lost their feeling of destiny. Instead, they learned the language of the nation in which they found themselves, adapted themselves to the culture, and asked no other privilege than a chance to prove their worthiness in the scheme of things.

If there is an occasional feeling of pride which helps to neutralize what could be qualms of despair, this, too, is part of your heritage. You are proud of your ancestry as you count the milestones along time's highway placed there by the many contributions Judaism has made in fields of philosophy, science, literature, and the arts; in modern technology, medicine, education, communication skills; in the expansion of cities, and the building of a nation. You are aware that your people have always remained true to their religion and that faithfully and realistically they have pursued the truth along a trail which has led from ancient Sinai, where the teaching was first received, to the newest synagogue, where it will continue to be taught. This trail, leading both ways, into the past and into the future, represents the adventurous journey of your people and you.

This is how you would feel, had you been born a Jew.

7

Had You Been Born
a Moslem

"IN THE NAME OF GOD, the Beneficent, the Merciful. . . ."
All over the world, five times each day, faithful worshipers kneel on prayer rugs, touch their foreheads to the ground,
and fervently murmur the words, "In the name of God, the
Beneficent, the Merciful. . . ."

Had you been born a Moslem, you would have learned the
prayer long before you grasped its full meaning. You would have
been told that it came from the Holy Koran, the most beloved
book in your parental home. This sacred scripture, considered to
be the most classical and perfect of all books in Arabic literature,
was dictated by the Angel Gabriel to an uneducated but chosen
man of God, the Prophet Mohammed.

This you would truly believe, had you been born a Moslem.
Like the 450,000,000 fellow members of your faith who believe as
you do, you kneel in prayer, facing toward the holy city of Mecca
in Hejaz, Arabia, and chant the impressive words, "In the name
of God, the Beneficent, the Merciful."

THE MEANING OF MOSLEM

You were taught that Moslem means: surrender to the will of God. It also means: one who accepts God and the Islamic faith. The word Islam refers to the religion itself, while Moslem (or Muslim) signifies the individual member. Sometimes non-Moslems refer to you as a Mohammedan. They mean that you are a follower of the Prophet Mohammed, which is true, but you and your people prefer to be called Moslem, a term sanctioned by Mohammed.

Had you been born a Moslem, you would consider yourself a link in an unbroken chain of tradition, the tradition of a people who were divided until Mohammed united them, a people who had no consolidating belief until Islam and its teachings welded them together. Through the inspiration and guidance of the Holy Koran, the warring tribes of Arabia became the "People of the Book" joined by the universal prayer:

"In the name of God, the Beneficent, the Merciful,
Praise be to God, Lord of the worlds,
The Beneficent, the Merciful,
Master of the day of requital.
Thee do we serve and thee do we beseech for help;
Guide us on the right path,
The path of those upon whom thou hast bestowed favors,
Not those upon whom wrath is brought down,
Nor those who go astray."

MOSQUES, MINARETS, AND THE CALL
OF THE MUEZZIN

In the village where you lived there were places associated with the prayer in a special way. These houses of God, which were the most beautiful and respected buildings in your community, were the mosques, a type of architecture introduced by Islam. These domed edifices expressed the highest artistry and workmanship of which your people were capable. Adjoining each house of worship is the minaret, a high tower with a circular platform near its very top. Onto this platform a man climbs five times daily. Silhouetted against the sky, he stands like a bearded prophet calling his people to worship. He is the muezzin, appointed to summon the faithful to prayer. Wearing a loose-fitting black robe and a green turban, he cups his hands and chants in a loud voice the unforgettable call:

"God is the Greatest, God is the Greatest,
I bear witness that there is only one God,
I bear witness that there is only one God;
I bear witness that Mohammed is the Prophet of God,
I bear witness that Mohammed is the Prophet of God,
Hasten to prayer, hasten to prayer;
Hasten to prosperity, hasten to prosperity;
God is the Greatest, God is the Greatest,
There is only one God."

Often when you heard the muezzin call out these words, you saw in your mind's eye your brother Moslems throughout the Middle East, Africa, Asia, Europe, and North America, listening to their muezzins and believing, as you believed, that God is very near and very personal. You saw them walking to their mosques to join in a fraternity of prayer to the God whose name is Allah. Allah is the Arabic word for the God who is worshiped by people of other religions as well as by Islam; the God who is the highest concept of all that is good, the Creator of all things and the Father who fills the earth with His love and His presence. Even though you knew this, how could you describe Him or explain His greatness? Islam tried to define Him when it said:

"God is one and has no partner;
Singular, without any like Him;
Uniform, having no contrary;
Separate, having no equal;
Ancient, having no first;
Eternal, having no beginning;
Everlasting, having no end;
Ever-existing, without termination;
Perpetual and constant, with neither interruption nor
termination;
Ever qualified with the attributes of supreme greatness;
Unbound and undetermined by lapse of ages or times;
The Alpha and Omega, the Evident and the Hidden."

Whenever you were asked to define or describe God or Allah, your mind filled with visions of worship; you saw the mosque and the minarets; you heard the call of the muezzin; you recalled the prayer out of the Holy Koran and you said, "Allah simply *is*, and everything that is, is Allah. Allah is God and God is one."

GOD ALONE IS WORTHY OF WORSHIP

One of your most thrilling memories is the time your father first took you to the mosque. He said, "Come, son, we are going to the house of God." He took your hand and together you walked to the center of the city where the great mosque stood and where people were reverently gathering. It was Friday, the Islamic Sabbath, which for your people is the "day of gathering." High on the minaret the muezzin was calling, *"La illah illa'llah! Mohammed rasulu'llah!"* (There is no God but Allah. Mohammed is His Prophet.) When you heard the words, "Hasten to prayer! Hasten to prayer!" spoken by the muezzin, you and your father hurried to join the others who were hastening to the square.

In an outer room you paused and removed your shoes. Your father explained, "This is a mark of respect to the house of God and to the worshipers who follow you in prayer. Shoes soil the lovely prayer rugs with which the floor of the mosque is covered, and it is on these rugs that the worshipers touch their foreheads when they pray."

Then you entered a room equipped with basins and water for your ablutions. You were told that no one ever goes into a mosque or says his prayers unless he is scrupulously clean. You washed your hands and your face, then your feet, and any other part of your body which you believed to be unclean. So it had been done in the days of Mohammed when the people washed themselves before worshiping, even while they were still wanderers in the desert and had no water. With nothing but the sparkling sand with which to cleanse themselves, they had complied with this ritual.

As you started toward the open doors which admitted you to the large, carpeted assembly room of the mosque, your father said, "Better than clean hands, my son, is a clean heart," which was his way of emphasizing that whoever comes to prayer should think clean thoughts and put every dishonest intention from his mind.

When you entered the prayer room, it was as though you stepped from the world of things into the presence of God. Beneath the great dome of the mosque your brother Moslems were gathering, but this day there were no women present. Sometimes there were services especially for women, but the Prophet had said, "It is more meritorious for a woman to say her prayers in her own house or in the courtyard of her house." You felt that in a very real way Islam was a man's religion, and as you knelt down, facing in the direction of Mecca, the birthplace of Mohammed, you were glad that you were a boy. When the murmur of the prayers rose around you like an enchanted chorus, filling you with a nearness to God, your heart was lifted up as if the prayers had wings. "O, you who believe!" said the Holy Koran, "when the call is made for prayer, endeavor to the remembrance of God!"

The words lingered in your mind as you knelt, lost among the rows upon rows of worshipers, and you bowed your forehead to the ground. As the men bent down in unison and raised themselves and bent down again, the rhythm seemed to you like the waves of the ocean, flooding your heart with Allah's love. Afterwards, as you listened to a sermon preached by the imam (minister) you realized that Islam is a religion of simple beauty which seeks to absorb the worshiper in the presence of God. There are no icons or statues or signs or symbols in this great room which is your church; there are no pews or chairs or musical instruments. The designs on the walls are geometric or floral which lead your thoughts ever more to Allah, making you want to say no more than can be said in the Koran's immortal words, "In the name of God, the Beneficent, the Merciful, praise be to God, Lord of the worlds!"

THE KORAN SPEAKS OF JESUS

As far as you are concerned, Mohammed was the greatest prophet of God, but you were taught and you accepted the fact that Jesus, as well as all other true prophets such as Adam, Noah, Abraham, Jacob, Moses, should be equally revered. The Holy

Koran says, "We believe in God, and that which hath been sent down to us, and that which hath been sent down to Abraham and Ishmael and Isaac and Jacob and the tribes; and that which was given to Moses and to Jesus, and that which was given to the prophets from their Lord. No difference do we make between any of them; and to God are we resigned."

Again the Koran says, "Some of the apostles we have endowed more highly than others; to some God hath spoken, and he hath raised others of them to the loftiest grade; and to Jesus, the son of Mary, we gave manifest proofs of his mission, and we strengthened him with the Holy Spirit."

But it also adds, "The Messiah (Jesus), son of Mary, is but an apostle; other apostles have flourished before him; and his mother was a just person; they both are good."

The Christian belief that Jesus was actually "God" walking on earth is difficult for you to understand. Equally difficult for you is the Christian concept that a loving God would demand the death of His son. Nor could you agree with the Christian view that man was "conceived and born in sin." Inherent in your faith is the belief that all men are born innocent and free. Sin is not inherited. It is acquired. Most of all, you often wonder why, if Jesus was really God, there should be so many divisions in Christendom. Some Christians insisted that the soul died with the body and would be raised when the physical body was restored; others claimed that the soul was immortal and went immediately to heaven or hell; some worshiped the Virgin Mary and were called Mariamites; still others said that Jesus had not actually died on the cross at all but had been whisked away by faithful followers before death came to him.

But there are also divisions among the people of Islam. There are Shiites, who believe that the successors to Mohammed must come directly from among the members of the Prophet's immediate family. They consider Ali, Mohammed's son-in-law, as the first rightful successor to the prophetship. Within the Shiite branch are the Ismailians, who follow an 8th century imam named Ismail. And there are Sunnites, representing the more orthodox wing of

Islam, who recognize the first four caliphs as the Prophet's true successors. These two divisions, the Shiites and the Sunnites, together with the mystical Sufis and other schools of thought, developed for the most part over the question of who should rule in Mohammed's place, and over differences in emphasis on pietistic practices.

These divisions never bothered you because you knew that all Moslems are united by the Holy Koran, which says, "There is no God but Allah. To Him shall be the final gathering." And all Moslems are united in their conviction that God divinely revealed Himself through Mohammed who taught his people the prayer, "In the name of God, the Beneficent, the Merciful. . . ."

A PROPHET IS BORN

Who was Mohammed and what was he like? He was born in 570 A.D. of poor parents and named, it is said, Ubu'l Kassim, although some authorities claim he was named Mohammed from birth. His father, who belonged to the Meccan tribe of Koraish, died two months before his son's birth. Six years later his mother also passed away, leaving the boy to be brought up by a grandfather, Abdul Muttalib, and later by an uncle, Abu Talib, who often took Ubu'l Kassim on caravan journeys to distant trading posts. Mecca, at this time (toward the close of the 6th century), was the commercial crossroads of the world, the thoroughfare between India and Persia, Syria and Greece, a place where travelers rested and merchants engaged in "international" trade. It was here, too, that Bedouins and other desert tribes came to sell their wares and satisfy their religious longings.

Religion was big business in Mecca. Here were shrines to 360 Arabian gods and goddesses. Here was Zemzem, the holy well, at which the followers of many gods drank of the water which was said to contain miraculous healing powers. Here in Mecca was the famous Black Stone. About the size of a pomegranate, it was oval in shape and approximately seven inches in diameter, very mysterious and, it was said, full of unexplained wonder. Long before the days of Mohammed, the Black Stone was an object of superstitious worship. Legend said that it had once been so purely white and so brilliant that pilgrims who came to the city were guided by its radiance.

Enshrined in a cube-like building called the Kaaba, the stone was watched over by relays of pagan priests. In those early days, fees were collected for prayers and promises of good luck, and there was so much commercialization of religion that, so it was said, the beautiful white stone turned black because of its displeasure over the sins of men. Though this was a myth, most people were convinced that the fabulous stone was the one which the Angel Gabriel had presented to the patriarch Abraham long ago.

The Kaaba is enclosed by a huge wall and is watched over by seven minarets. It is said that in the days of Mohammed there were temples dedicated to the seven planets and that various Arabian tribes had specified certain planets as their guardian deities. Many households also had their sacred images, either in the form of a planet-god or a nature-spirit, representing certain cosmic forces. Judaism and early Christianity sought to make an inroad into this idolatry and had converted several tribes to their faiths.

Christian and Jewish thought, as well as the mystery and magic of Zoroastrianism and the philosophy and practices of Hinduism were all part of the confused religious scene in Mecca. The cries of vendors of religious articles, the chanted prayers of Arabian priests, and the incessant voices of beggars seeking alms in the name of numerous gods shocked Ubu'l Kassim whenever he returned to the city of his birth. He had an affection for the Kaaba as most people had, for there was a belief that before the creation of the world, a prototype of the Kaaba had been built in heaven and that Abraham and his son, Ishmael, erected this one in Mecca, directly under the heavenly spot where the eternal Kaaba is supposed to stand.

A legend tells how once when the sacred temple of the Kaaba was to be rebuilt, the question arose as to who should have the honor of replacing the Black Stone in its sacred niche. Because each tribe argued that it should have this great privilege, a priest advised the disputants to choose as their judge the first man who entered through a certain gate. The tribes agreed and, after several moments, a man appeared. It was Ubu'l Kassim, who later became the Prophet Mohammed. After he had considered the problem, he suggested that the stone be placed on a piece of cloth so that each tribe could share the honor of bearing the stone to its holy place.

It is possible that Ubu'l Kassim often thoughtfully placed his own offerings around the sacred stone just as did other worshipers. But more than any other seeker after truth, he hoped and prayed that the true God would reveal Himself. For this reason he frequently retired to the desert or to a cave in a mount outside the city of Mecca for meditation and prayer.

At the age of twenty-five he was described as being a serious-minded, generous and competent man, although he had never learned to read or write. He was handsome and commanding in appearance, a red-bearded man with fair skin and piercing black eyes, whose luxurious hair was usually hidden inside a large green turban. To this day the green turban is worn by the descendants of Mohammed, while black, red, and yellow turbans represent Dervish sects which are dedicated to a life of poverty and strict adherence to Islam.

At twenty-five, Ubu'l Kassim married a wealthy widow named Khadijah, a member of the Koreishite clan. Though she was twelve years his senior, the marriage proved singularly happy and their home life was an example of harmony and peace. Khadijah was blessed with seven children, among them Ali, the prophet's favorite son, and Fatimah, believed by the Shiites to represent the highest ideal of womanhood.

GOD CALLS HIS PROPHET

One evening as Ubu'l Kassim went up to the sandy cave on Mount Hira and looked out over the city of Mecca, his heart filled with compassion and grief for his people. He was now nearly forty years old. The Arab world was still hopelessly divided into warring tribes and separated by many religions and superstitions. Utterly alone, he resorted to prayer, as he had many times before, longing for a vision of the true God. There were no statues in the cave as there were around the Kaaba, no priests, no famous stone. There was only this seeker of Truth who, kneeling with his forehead to the damp earth, said, "O God, fill me with thy Presence and teach me who and what You truly are."

He remained there for a long time, wrapped in his cloak, as he had done throughout other nights. But suddenly a great light surrounded him, bursting upon the mountain with a brightness that spread across the sky. When he saw it, he cried out, "Allah—God!"

A voice said to him, "Read!"

"I cannot read," he said.

A second and a third time the voice ordered, "Read!"

"What shall I read?" he asked, and then it seemed to him that there were words all around him, living words written on the overhanging walls of the cave.

"Read," the voice insisted, and then as if to assist him, said, "In the name of Allah who created man from a clot, and thy Lord the Most Bounteous who teacheth by the pen, teacheth man that which he knew not. Read: Verily is man rebellious. He thinketh himself independent. Lo! Unto thy Lord is the return!"

"Who are you? Let me see your face!" he cried.

"I am Gabriel," said the voice.

In a vision, the Angel appeared before him, standing in space and holding in his hands a silken shawl covered with words of gold. Mohammed recognized them as the words he earlier had been asked to read. No matter which way he turned, the Angel was there before him, and the voice said, "O, Mohammed! Thou art the Prophet of Allah, the most high God!" Then the vision ended and the voice was stilled.

THE TEST OF FAITH

Mohammed rushed from the cave. Could it have been a dream, he wondered? Had someone tricked him? God had been a mystery for so long that now the thought that He might be understood was greatly disturbing. He hurried home following old familiar paths which now seemed strangely new.

When he saw Khadijah, he cried out, "Wrap me up, wrap me

up!" His wife, alarmed by his great agitation, brought him a garment and made him sit before the fire. When he had told her his story, she said, "Rejoice and be cheerful, for God has chosen you to be His prophet to His people."

Khadijah then told her cousin, Waraqa, a blind, aged scholar of both Christianity and Judaism. Waraqa said, "Verily, this is the Holy Spirit that revealed Himself to Moses." Then the blind man spoke to Mohammed directly, "They will persecute you, they will banish you, and seek to kill you. Oh, that I could live to fight for you!"

Khadijah and Waraqa, the first converts to Islam, never doubted that God had revealed Himself to Mohammed. But as the days went by and the Angel Gabriel failed to reappear, Mohammed often despaired. People who watched the strongly-built, red-bearded man walk out beyond the city said, "He still goes to the cave in Mount Hira. What does he hope to find?"

One day, however, he did not go to the cave, but went instead to a towering cliff. He stood there looking for a long time into the sky. When he tried to pray, tears filled his eyes. He gazed down into the deep valley. Surely, he told himself, the vision in the cave must have been the sorcery of the evil one. How could God be found? How was it possible for a man ever to break through the veil that separated truth from illusion? Despair swept over him. Something told him to end it all by throwing himself over the cliff. Just as he started forward, a blinding light burst over him and before him stood the Angel Gabriel with upraised hand. Mohammed bowed his forehead to the ground. Then a voice from heaven commanded, "O thou, wrapped in thy mantle, rise up and glorify thy God!"

After this experience the Prophet never doubted God again, even though his faith was tested time after time. Again and again the Angel Gabriel appeared to him in heavenly visitations, dictating to Mohammed by way of inspiration the treasured suras (chapters) which were to make up the Holy Koran.

HOW THE HOLY KORAN WAS WRITTEN

On the coldest days and the darkest nights, Mohammed,

wrapped in his cloak, sat with his eyes closed, an instrument of Allah, making known Allah's will to men. While beads of sweat covered his face and dropped from his beard, he repeated aloud the words which Gabriel put into his heart. A hundred and fourteen *suras,* containing nearly 80,000 words, were dictated by him as the mouthpiece of God. These were copied down by friends and relatives either at the exact moment or later, because often the spirit of inspiration would come upon the Prophet when he was walking about or engaged in his work. Through the years, fragments were copied down upon stones or pieces of leather or upon palm leaves and then faithfully compiled. Chief among the recorders of Mohammed's words were his cousin Ali, his close friend Abu Bekr, and an amanuensis named Zaid Ibn Thabit. Skeptics also came to hear the Prophet's words, and often they went away convinced that Allah was indeed speaking through His chosen one.

These early converts saw what many non-believers did not see. They saw that God had called an unschooled messenger to be an instrument of His will. They saw in Mohammed not the fanatical, demented man many accused him of being, but a man destined for a great mission. They realized that Allah had no need of images or priests; Allah had need only of the trance-like figure of the bearded Prophet, through whom He could reveal His word.

The Holy Koran became that word, the very heart of Islam. Because its recitation was considered one of the most distinguished marks of faith and learning, many early converts memorized the entire book. He who was best versed in the Koran was usually called upon to conduct public prayers and to speak on the meaning of Islam. To this very day, he who knows the Koran is held in the highest possible esteem among Moslems throughout the world. For it is believed that no one can memorize the Holy Koran without having his life affected and changed.

This inspired scripture speaks of many things. It tells its people that no one can atone for sins excepting the sinner himself. It assures its readers that God will not burden any man beyond his ability to carry the burden. It insists that no individual is held responsible for evil thoughts which pass through his mind, nor is he condemned for mistakes that he does not honestly know to be wrong.

It sets forth Six Principles of Faith:

1. God is one, and this one is Allah.

2. God's angels are God's messengers and aids, and there are evil spirits to oppose them.

3. God sent his prophets to earth at stated times and for stated purposes. The last and greatest of these is Mohammed.

4. The Holy Koran is Allah's truly inspired book, and all the books of God—Jewish and Christian scriptures—are also holy.

5. The Day of Judgment will find good and evil deeds weighed in the balance and all souls will pass to heaven or to hell on a bridge finer than a hair and sharper than a sword.

6. The lives and acts of men are foreordained by an all-knowing God.

Because of the Koran and its holy Prophet, you try to live according to the Five Pillars of the Faith which say,

1. Recite the *shahadah* daily which says, "There is no God but Allah; Mohammed is the messenger of Allah."

2. Pray the *salat* or daily prayer five times daily, facing Mecca.

3. Give the *zakat* or tithe toward the expansion of Islam and the support of the poor.

4. Observe Ramadan, the ninth month of the Moslem calendar, during which a fast is kept during the daylight hours as a commemoration of the first revelation of the Koran.

5. Make a pilgrimage to Mecca if your finances and your health allow, and pay your homage to Allah at the Holy Kaaba.

And you seek to obey the warnings and admonitions of the Holy Koran which implore you not to steal, not to lie, not to speak evil of anyone, not to indulge in intoxication or other bodily sin, and not to worship idols of any kind.

THE PROPHET'S MISSION

Mohammed's mission was to proclaim the unity of God to a people who were worshiping many gods, to emphasize personal responsibility in the matter of faith, and to warn men that judgment awaited them in the life to come. Any one of these pronouncements would have set the priests of Mecca against him; together they called forth ridicule and threats from both pagan priests and pagan people. Opposition to Mohammed was fanned by the keepers of the Kaaba, but despite this, or perhaps because of it, the Prophet's converts increased.

Often he stood at the very entrance of the Kaaba and preached his gospel of the One God and the Holy Book. When Abu Talib warned him of his danger and of the growing hatred, Mohammed said, "O, my uncle, if they placed the sun in my right hand and the moon in my left, to cause me to renounce my task, verily I would not desist until God made manifest His cause or I perished in the attempt."

So his converts grew and the Meccan priests said, "What will happen to us if people forsake our gods and follow the One God of Mohammed? Surely the whole business world of Mecca will be destroyed." They watched his popularity increase. They heard his pronouncements grow more bold. They realized that the secular kingdom was being threatened by the kingdom of Allah, so they laid a plot to kill this fanatical Prophet of the Lord. Throughout Mecca the pagan hierarchy appointed numerous men bound by oath to take Mohammed's life.

Appearing in a vision, the Angel Gabriel warned Mohammed of his danger, advising him to urge his followers to leave the city and to seek refuge wherever they could. Then, on the night appointed for his death, Mohammed, together with Ali and Abu Bekr, remained in the city after all other Moslems had fled. The assassins came at midnight. They surrounded the house, never suspecting that the power of Allah might be greater than the force and terror of their swords. They saw the door open but, according to one legend, that was all they saw, for when Mohammed appeared, Allah struck the would-be murderers with blindness. Numb with fright, they begged for mercy, and Mohammed walked through their ranks scattering dust upon their heads as he passed by. Seemingly as God willed, their blindness was only temporary, a protective shield by which Allah saved his messenger.

Another account describes how the murderous mob watched through a hole in the door while the Prophet slept. Their instructions had been to kill him the moment he left the house. The Prophet, however, had directed Ali to lie down in his place, wrapped in the Prophet's cloak, while Mohammed had already escaped unseen through a window.

However the miraculous escape may have been made, it was Allah who arranged the deliverance. It was Allah who guided Mohammed unharmed to the home of Abu Bekr and then to a cave in Mount Thor, southeast of Mecca. It was Allah who protected His Prophet for three days in the refuge of a cave. Some insist that Abu Bekr was with him, while others say that he was accompanied only by a servant. It is related that after Mohammed took refuge in the cave, two doves laid their eggs at the entrance and a spider covered the mouth of the cave with its web, which prevented the enemies of the Prophet of God from detecting Mohammed's hiding place.

Once when a band of murderers came so near that the servant began to despair, Mohammed said, "Fear not. Allah is with us."

"And," says an inclusion in the Holy Koran, "Allah caused His peace of reassurance to descend upon him and supported him with hosts ye cannot see and made the word of those who disbelieved the nethermost, while Allah's word became the uppermost. Allah is Mighty, Wise!"

On the night that Mohammed fled from Mecca, July 2, 622 A.D., a new religious era dawned upon the world. Islam reckons time from the period of this flight, just as Christians begin their era from the year of Christ's birth. Christians speak of contemporary events as occurring in A.D. (Anno Domini), the year of the Lord; Moslems refer to them as occurring in A.H. (Anno Hegira), the year of the Prophet's flight.

TRIUMPH OF ISLAM

The Prophet fled to Medina, where the people welcomed him and great crowds flocked to learn from him. For seven years he was looked upon as an inspired religious and political leader. Two rival tribes which had long been engaged in bitter warfare found him to be their mediator. Mohammed united them, and under his influence Medina was so transformed in its faith and morals that even today it is called "the city of the Prophet."

His first official act was to build and dedicate a mosque; his first important program was to teach the people the Holy Koran. His first document which united the people began, "In the name of the Most Merciful and Compassionate God, this charter is given by Mohammed, the Apostle of God, to all believers. . . ."

With Medina as the base of operations, Mohammed tried many times to conquer Mecca. Great campaigns were lodged against the city and there was extensive loss of life, but even with failure the Prophet's following grew and his leadership became more established. On January 1, 630 A.D., he surrounded himself with 10,000 men and once more marched against the "idolatrous city." This time he was met by a Meccan delegation which had been dispatched to negotiate terms of peace or persuade him to give up his campaign. When the leader of the delegation, Abu Sofian, confronted Mohammed, the latter said, "You ask me to abandon my plans. Has not the time come, O Abu Sofian, for you to acknowledge that there is no God but Allah, and that I am His Prophet?" At this Abu Sofian knelt down, touched his forehead to the ground, and embraced the faith of Islam.

Almost unopposed, the Prophet entered the city of his birth. Seated on his favorite camel, Al Kaswa, and with Abu Bekr riding next to him, he proclaimed Mecca henceforth to be the holiest city of Islam and dedicated it to the glory of God.

Critics of Islam say that Mohammed changed from a spiritual leader to a military dictator whose armies were to sweep across

Egypt, Persia, and Greece, converting nations by means of the sword. You, however, see him as a man sent by God to crush evil and immorality and to destroy idolatry at any cost. You believe he entered Mecca with a prayer on his lips, and that the first thing he did was to give thanks to God for victory. You believe he circled the Kaaba seven times, that he destroyed the 360 images, and that with each shattering blow he cried, "God is great! Truth has come and falsehood is destroyed!" All that followed was part of destiny and the fulfillment of God's immortal plan.

Each year following the conquest, Mohammed came to Mecca from Medina to lead his people in a pilgrimage to the holy Kaaba where they bowed before the only symbol of Islam: the Sacred Stone. In 632 A.D. at the age of sixty-two, when he said that this would be his farewell pilgrimage, more than 100,000 of the faithful walked with him in one of the most solemn marches ever made. At the Kaaba they worshiped together. Then Mohammed preached to them, predicting his death. He concluded his sermon by saying, "O God, I have fulfilled my message and accomplished my work!" To which the great multitude replied, "Yea, verily thou hast!" He returned to Medina and there are many tender recollections which Moslems have handed down from generation to generation concerning the Prophet's final days. The last time he appeared in the mosque, he said to the people, "O Moslems, if I have wronged any one of you, here I am to answer for it. If I owe aught to anyone, all I may happen to possess belongs to you." At this an old man arose and claimed that he once had given three coins to a poor man at the request of the Prophet. Mohammed immediately paid him the coins and said, "It is better to blush in this world than in the next."

On the day that word spread throughout Medina that the Prophet had died, faithful Moslems refused to believe it. Some insisted that Allah's chosen ones could never die. Mohammed's beloved wife, Khadijah, had passed away, to be sure, and he had mourned for her. Later, in keeping with Arabic custom, he had remarried—had married several women, as was permitted—and his favorite wife was young Aisha. Now Aisha herself confirmed the Prophet's death. She described how she had held his aged head in her arms as he lay on his sick bed. She reported how she saw him suddenly rise up and stare into the distance. She said she heard him whisper three times, "Gabriel, come close to me!" She was convinced that the Angel himself had come to escort him into the life beyond.

Listening to Aisha's account, the people were deeply affected. But the fact of Mohammed's passing was accepted only after the faithful Abu Bekr went into the room where the Prophet lay, kissed the dead man's forehead, and came out to address the huge, excited throngs.

"O people!" Abu Bekr cried, "as for you who used to worship Mohammed, Mohammed is dead. But as for you who used to worship Allah, Allah is alive and dieth not. Does not the Holy Koran say, 'Mohammed is but a messenger, messengers the like of whom have passed away before him'? Will it be that, when he dieth, ye will turn back on your heels? He who turneth back doth not hurt Allah, and Allah will reward the thankful!"

There was some dispute between the various tribes as to where the Prophet should be buried, but Abu Bekr affirmed that Mohammed himself had once said that a prophet should be buried at the very spot on which he passed away. Accordingly, a grave was dug beneath the room in the house where Mohammed had died. Here his body was washed, perfumed, wrapped in a white shroud and lovingly laid to rest.

RELIGION DICTATES SOCIAL CUSTOMS

Though Mohammed died, the faith of Islam was never to die, and the customs established by the religion were to change slowly if at all. The Holy Koran had dictated precepts for the individual and social life of its people and had enumerated many instructions in the matter of worship and prayer. It prohibited the use of intoxicating liquor, the eating of pork and the practice of gambling, and enjoined upon its followers the absolute keeping of one's word. It forbade adultery and commanded complete obedience to Allah's precepts.

These precepts Mohammed himself faithfully observed and

from his life you and the people of Islam take inspiration. You picture him as a frugal, hard-working man who wove his own cloth, made his own garments and cobbled his own shoes. You cite many minute details of his life and habits: whenever he spoke to someone he faced the person fully and uprightly; whenever he shook hands, he was never the first to withdraw his hand, nor the first to break off a conversation. He hated nothing more than lying, and loved nothing better than kindliness. He had a temper that flared easily, but he learned to discipline it and keep himself in hand, believing that a man must first master himself before he can presume to master others.

Had you been born a Moslem, you would understand the polygamous life of the Prophet and interpret it differently than most non-Moslems are wont to do. You would point out that for nearly thirty years he remained married to one wife, Khadijah, even though Arabian custom would have permitted him many wives. It was only after the death of Khadijah that he created his harem of nine wives, and, as everyone knew, his household was considered an example of virtuous living. The records of Islam show that his relationship with his wives was above suspicion of sensuality. He lived with them in a row of humble cottages, adobe huts, the doors of which were strips of leather. His attitude toward the women of his seraglio was quiet and subdued, for the Holy Koran had ordered that family life should be the embodiment of justice and love.

The Koran had put a sanction upon the Prophet's household when it said, "We have made lawful unto thee thy wives unto whom thou hast paid their dowries, and those whom thy right hand possesseth of those whom Allah hath given thee as spoils of war."

Non-Moslems might read into these words whatever they wished. You are convinced of the rightness of the Prophet's views and the infallible statutes of the Holy Koran. You remember how Aisha described Mohammed's personal habits: "He divides each day into three portions. The first portion of each day is given to God, the second to his family, and the third to his people." Because he loved freedom, he freed his slaves. Because he wished to be no better than other men, he put away the rings and jewels which devotees had given him.

The life and the pronouncements of the Prophet became customs for Islam and for you. Once Mohammed said, "There are four things which, if a person is endowed with any of them, bless the individual and the world. *First, a heart that is grateful; second, a tongue that utters constantly the name of God; third, a mind that is patient and calm amid troubles; fourth, a wife that is never guilty of a breach of trust, either in respect of her own person or in respect of her husband's property."*

MOSLEM MARRIAGES

In some Islamic countries even today, Moslem men have several wives. Occasionally the wives are heavily veiled, as was the custom also among early Syrian Christians. Sometimes wives are in *purdah,* which means they appear in public completely covered from head to foot in a tentlike garment which has only a narrow aperture for the eyes. The Holy Koran does not order such extreme veiling, but it is believed by some that the custom originated from instructions concerning the behavior of men who wished to speak to the wives of the Prophet. They were ordered to do this only through a curtain. "That," observes the Koran, "is purer for your hearts and for their hearts." But whether the practice of *purdah* came from the Islamic faith or from some more ancient source, it has long been a part of Moslem tradition and is only now slowly giving way to change.

Marriage in Islam is both a civil contract and a sacrament. At the time of your marriage you and your partner would be asked to make a public declaration and have two witnesses attest that the marriage is of your own free will and that the contract has been concluded. Then following this simple form, the religious or sacred contract would take place, also in a simple ceremony with or without an imam officiating. Festivities are added to the wedding plans in accordance with the wishes and social status of the parties. These observances vary all the way from the elaborate weddings of the late Aly Khan, who was head of the Ismaili sect, to the lowly marriage of a humble Saudi Bedouin who served each of his guests one date and one small cup of black coffee.

At your wedding, parents, relatives, and friends would be invited to the house of the bride. Here the imam opens the service by reading from the Holy Koran. Then he delivers a brief sermon embellished with many wise admonitions.

"Among my followers," Mohammed once said, "the best of men are they who are best to their wives, and the best of women are they who are best to their husbands. . . .

"Verily, God exalts the position of a man in heaven, because his wife was pleased with him and prayed for him.

"Paradise lies at the feet of mothers. . . .

"Fear God in regard to the treatment of your wives, for verily they are your helpers. You have taken them on the security of God, and made them lawful by the words of God.

"She is the ideal wife who pleases thee when thou lookest at her, obeys thee when thou givest her direction; and protects her honor and thy property when thou art away.

"Verily, of all believers he has the most perfect faith who has the best manners, and shows the greatest kindness to his wife and children."

The imam then inquires whether anyone has any objection to the marriage. There being none, he appoints four men to approach the bride and ask if it is her wish and will to marry the groom. The groom makes his own statement publicly. Satisfied that the couple wish to be married of their own free will, by having consulted the four interrogators on this point, the imam stands for a moment solemnly in prayer. Then he says to the assembled people, "Did you hear what the witnesses and the groom have said?" And the people answer, "Yes."

Then the bride is "given away" by her father or a relative, and the marriage vows are repeated. Sometimes a ring is used, particularly in western countries. In most Islamic countries, the matter of a dowry still pertains and the father or guardian of the bride, as well as the groom, are called to the imam's side to sign the dowry contract. When this is done the imam says, "Al-Fatihah," (let us pray) and once again you hear the impressive words, "In the name of God, the Beneficent, the Merciful," following which the imam pronounces the couple man and wife.

Generally speaking a Moslem wife retains her distinct individuality after her marriage and need never assume her husband's name. This is a custom followed by Christians also in certain countries of the Middle East.

In the event of a divorce, the Islamic laws are very clear in providing for the protection of the wife's property against any avarice on the part of the husband. Islam says, "If the divorce is due to a cause imputable to the husband, he has to make over to her all her property, and pay off the dowry that had been settled upon her. If, however, the divorce has been resorted to at the instance of the wife, without any justifiable cause, she has simply to abandon her claim to the dowry."

A divorce may be granted for: 1) habitual ill-treatment of a marriage partner; 2) non-fulfillment of the terms of the marriage contract; 3) insanity; 4) incurable incompetency; 5) desertion; 6) other causes which in the opinion of a court of law justify a separation.

Occasionally the imam is consulted in the matter of marital difficulties, but his position is not as important in Islam as is the place of the priest in Catholicism or the rabbi in Judaism. In some Moslem villages problems are solved by the imam, but his capacity is mainly that of a teacher and a leader of the services in the mosque.

Children may be blessed by the imam if the parents so desire, but this is not considered a sacramental act as it is in the Christian faith. Circumcision is practiced among Moslems for reasons that vary all the way from hygienic justification to an early mark of tribal affiliation. The rite is often performed by professional men who make this their business, by a physician or, in rare cases, by the imam himself.

But there is one circumstance when a Moslem, at whatever time, and wherever he may be, calls upon the imam for special comfort and wisdom. This is at the time of a death in the family.

DEATH IS A TIME APPOINTED

Had you been born a Moslem, you would have a deep conviction that every individual's time on earth is foreordained. You believe with all your heart the words of the Holy Koran which say, "No one can die except by God's purpose, according to the Book that fixeth the term of life." You have been taught that, "Nothing can befall us, but what God hath ordained." These thoughts flood your mind when a loved one passes away, and if you are with someone at the time of his death, you say, "May God grant that we meet in the garden of Allah! God grant that you and I eat together from the fruits of Paradise." It is something of a custom for Moslems to believe that the dying one, if he can speak, will say something like this, "Forgive me in whatever I have failed."

A burial rite in the Moslem faith is marked by dignified simplicity. The body is washed, perfumed, and wrapped in a new white cloth. This shroud must be seamless and must cover the body from head to feet. The funeral service usually takes place in the home or in a mortuary, although sometimes the ceremony is observed in the mosque. The departed one is placed on a bier and carried on the shoulders of loved ones to his final resting place. Many Moslems believe that bands of angels follow the procession to the grave. Although today in Islam, as in most faiths, there is frequently a motorized funeral cortege, Moslems remember that the Prophet Mohammed always walked when he was among the mourners in a funeral procession. He was lost in thought whenever he attended the burial of a loved one, as though he were himself communing with the angels. And because angels were very real to him, they are to most Moslems. Some believe that four mighty archangels are near to earth at the time a loved one dies. It is then that Gabriel, the angel of revelations, and Michael, the angel of rain, and Azrail, the angel of death, and Israfil, the angel of resurrection, walk with those who mourn.

When the body is laid to rest and the grave is sealed, the imam sits near the head of the grave and recites the *talqueen* which consists of questions and answers which, it is believed, the deceased is asking as he rests in his tomb. According to Mohammed, when an adult is placed in the grave, he encounters two angels, Nakir and Munkir, who come to hear the dead person's report. These angels question the deceased on the status of his faith and demand to know whether he believes in the unity of Allah and the mission of the Prophet. But actually this ritual has a deeper meaning than this, for the imam's *talqueen* is a reminder to those present that their souls will one day also be interrogated and that it is not only knowledge of Islamic truths, but also the deeds of the Islamic life which will judge a person on that final day. The *talqueen* is a warning to the living that all mortal men must one day face their encounter with Allah. It is also a warning to people that no one has perfectly fulfilled either the love of God or the love for man, and that mercy is a factor in all man's dealings. Therefore, the imam recites a prayer to the soul of the dead and then everyone says, "I forgive the beloved dead and ask him to forgive me. May the mercy of Allah be on him and on us."

The final hope is in the resurrection. You believe that both body and soul will some day be miraculously raised up and renewed. Just how and when this will happen is a mystery known only to God, but on the day of resurrection all mankind and all animals will be summoned to give an account of their actions. The Holy Koran is very clear and eloquent on the subject of life after death, and though Moslems may be divided politically and culturally, and though they may dispute about which sect is the true successor to the undefiled teachings of the Prophet, they are all united in the teachings of the holy book.

ISLAM AND YOU

To you, Islam is a great and beautiful religion and you would not change it for any other. You believe it is a world faith which draws no color lines and makes no distinctions between rich and poor. Whenever you meet a fellow Moslem you say, *"Salaam Alikum,"* which means "Peace be upon you." You are continually challenged by the faith of your fathers and by your love of God to recite your daily prayers, to attend the services in the mosque, and to teach the rules and principles of Islam to your children.

You look forward to the day when you will be able to make your pilgrimage to the holy city of Mecca. Should your circum· stances permit such a journey, or *hadj*, you would reverently enter the sacred portals of Mecca, put on a seamless gown, and walk in prayer seven times around the Kaaba as Mohammed did during his moment of conquest. You would stand where the Prophet stood and bow in prayer where once he prayed, and perhaps kiss the sacred Stone in his memory. When you returned to your home, many people would call you a *hadji*, that is, one who has made the great pilgrimage and who has rededicated his life to Allah and Islam.

Yours is a religion of joy and submission, a vital, moving, logical faith which throughout its history of triumph and tears has never doubted or criticized the will of God. Your greatest wish is to be worthy of the teaching of the Holy Koran; your greatest delight is when you gather your children around you and say, "Come, 1 will teach you the prayer my father taught me when he said, 'In the name of God, the Beneficent, the Merciful. Praise be to God, Lord of the worlds, the Beneficent, the Merciful, Master of the day of Requital.' "

This, to you, would be the Lord's Prayer of Islam, and the fulfillment of your faith, had you been born a Moslem.

8

Had You Been Born
a Roman Catholic

THE CATHOLIC CHURCH IS MANY THINGS. It is a mystical body of believers in Jesus Christ. It is an extension of the spiritual fellowship which Christ founded upon St. Peter. It is a channel of grace for all who believe. It is a visible organization whose headquarters are in the Vatican and whose leader, the Holy Father, represents the Vicar of Christ on earth. It is the Holy Ghost at work in the world; renewing, redeeming, restoring mankind to its rightful place in the community of God. It is the church universal, but, most of all, it is your spiritual home, had you been born a Roman Catholic.

CATHOLICISM IS THE CHURCH UNIVERSAL

All over the world Catholicism has built its churches and surmounted them with its most precious symbol: the cross of Christ. With few exceptions, every church edifice bears this emblem, usually on its tallest spires, the steeple or dome or campanile, reaching toward the sky. In many lands where your faith has conquered pagan cultures, churches were built where heathen shrines once stood, and the cross now looms where non-Christian religions once held sway.

You are at home whenever and wherever you step inside a Catholic church. Whether it is a city cathedral or a jungle chapel, there is a feeling about it that assures you of a Presence. You hear it in the silence, you sense it in the reverence with which worshipers come and go, you recognize it in the customs universally observed and, most of all, you find it in the awareness that here the spirit of the Lord has been enshrined through acts of worship, love, and faith.

Near you, as you enter, is the holy water fount. Whether it is a marble basin resting in the sculptured arms of an angelic image or a tiny porcelain container tacked beside a chapel door, the meaning is the same. You dip your fingers in the water and make the sign of the cross, touching your forehead, chest, left shoulder and then right shoulder. As you make this sign you are assured that there is a community of more than 500,000,000 people throughout the world who understand this salutary act. Regardless of color, station in life, virtues or sins, those who make this blessing know its deep significance. It is a reminder that Christ died upon the cross to redeem your soul. The holy water—water which the priest has blessed and to which a bit of salt has been added as a symbol of everlasting life—reminds you that before you enter into the presence of God you must cleanse your heart of evil and become purified in word and deed.

When you see the altar which dominates each Catholic church, you genuflect because of the Presence which you sense is localized here. Even when there is no service being observed and when you have just stepped into the church for a moment of meditation and prayer, you know the altar is a holy place. It contains the relic of a saint and conceals the consecrated Host which is exposed to view during Benediction, a brief ceremony of praise to this Blessed Sacrament. You believe that the Host represents the actual presence of God and it is small wonder, therefore, that you and all Catholics regard these surroundings as especially holy.

Here in the sacred precincts of your church you enter a pew and kneel to pray. Everything around you is conducive to worship: statues remind you of the presence of the saints, and a perpetually burning light near the altar assures you that God is the votive flame persisting in your faith.

On the walls around you are fourteen "stations of the cross," art works representing fourteen phases of the experiences through which Jesus passed on the *via dolorosa,* the way of sorrow, when He walked to Golgotha. Near the communion rail, which encloses the altar, candles have been lighted by faithful worshipers who have remembered a loved one or who, out of reverence, have left a burning candle as a lingering presence of themselves here in the church.

The worshipers around you also contribute to the sanctity of worship, for they have come seeking the same Presence which has drawn you here. Customarily, women enter with covered heads, and men, of course, remove their hats. In all the world, no surroundings are endowed with the reverence which your people show to the church, and in most localities, churches are open day and night for those who seek the solemn quiet of this house of prayer.

THE ROSARY

To assist you in your devotion and to help you meditate upon the mysteries of redemption, you frequently use a string of beads popularly called the Rosary. The use of beads as an aid to concentration is an ancient practice in many religions. In your faith their employment goes back to about the tenth century. Rosaries have fifty-five (sometimes fifty-nine) beads, with a small crucifix affixed.

It is customary for you, when you feel the need for worship, to take the beads in your hand and meditate upon the fifteen mysteries or events in the life of Mary and Jesus: *the Annunciation, the Visitation, the Nativity, the Presentation of Jesus in the Temple, the Discovery of Jesus in the Temple at the age of twelve, the Agony, the Scourging, the Crowning with Thorns, the Carrying of the Cross, the Crucifixion, the Resurrection, the Ascension, the Descent of the Holy Spirit, the Assumption, and the Corona-*

tion of the Blessed Virgin. You recite the "Hail Marys," repeating an "Our Father" between each set of ten as you meditate upon these mysteries and seek to mingle your life with the life of the Blessed Virgin and the Christ.

The real meaning of the Rosary, as far as you are concerned, is inherent in the *experience* of the recitation. You treasure it because of its sentimental symbology, but its purpose could be fulfilled without the actual Rosary itself. Yet, as you think about it, the beads themselves are very much a part of your life. When you were a child your mother used to give you a Rosary to play with long before you realized its meaning. Sometimes the thought comes to you that as a little child reaches out for its mother's hand and begs for support, so you reach for your Rosary and hold fast to it. The symbolic joy of divine affection, like the warmth of a mother's love, glows in your heart as you "count" the beads. You address the Blessed Virgin familiarly as one who loves her when you say, "Hail Mary, full of grace, blessed art thou among women, and blessed is the fruit of thy womb, Jesus." Boldly and confidently, you mention her exalted station, "Holy Mary, Mother of God." You beg her intercession for the life of your soul and the souls of all her other children when you recite the words, "Pray for us sinners now and at the hour of our death."

The Rosary is repeated in your home as part of your family worship. It is often recited at special services in the church, at wakes when someone has died, and even on special radio programs when a priest repeats the meaningful prayers and the faithful followers chant them with him. The Rosary, as a string of beads and as a prayer, would be a most precious part of your faith, had you been born a Roman Catholic.

THE AUTHORITY OF THE CHURCH

Often as you kneel in prayer or as you meditate upon your relationship with God, your heart fills with a sense of supreme assurance that among the world's many and often conflicting religions, your Church is founded upon infallible truth and endowed by God with divine authority. *You believe that to your Church has been entrusted the obligation of bringing to men the true doctrine of Christ through the Holy Spirit which works through the Catholic Church.* If this function seems to take on a legalistic tone, it is because Christ empowered His Church with truth, decreed how this truth should be expounded and directed how it should be administered throughout the world.

From earliest childhood you were taught in your home, in your parochial school and in your Church that Jesus Christ was the divine Son of God, miraculously born of the Blessed Virgin Mary and manifesting in His life, death, and resurrection the will and wish of God for the salvation of men. Among His disciples, who were chosen to perpetuate His teaching and commissioned to preach His gospel, was one upon whom primacy was bestowed. This was St. Peter, to whom Jesus said, "Thou art Peter and upon this rock I will build my Church, and the gates of hell shall not prevail against it. And I will give to thee the keys of the kingdom of heaven. And whatsoever thou shalt bind upon earth, it shall be bound also in heaven; and whatsoever thou shalt loose upon earth, it shall be loosed also in heaven." (Matthew 16:18,19)

This promise was not to end with the death of St. Peter, but was ordained to continue to the end of time through his legitimate successors. Peter was the first pope, and all others of them, through the changing years up to the present pope and all who come after him, are vested with this primacy. The very fact that the Church exists today in this unbroken continuity, despite all the vicissitudes through which it has passed, is proof to you of its divinity and a testimony to its divine mission in the world.

The supernatural authority attending this apostolic succession is evidenced in many ways. For example, the pope is infallible when he defines a doctrine on faith and morals *ex cathedra.* This means that he must speak as the Holy Ghost gives him utterance. It also means that there are four conditions involved: 1) the pronouncement must be made by him as the supreme teacher; 2) the subject matter must concern faith and morals; 3) the judgment which he hands down must command intellectual assent; 4) the definition must be impartially imparted to the whole body of the faithful. Such is papal infallibility. There is also Church infallibility, which extends beyond faith and morals to include the whole body of revealed truth, most impressively represented in religious rites called sacraments.

THE SACRAMENTS

A sacrament is a channel of divine grace imperative in effecting conformity with Christ. It is also the means through which certain profound truths are articulated and by the use of which the power of Christ is perpetuated in the lives of individuals and the world. The sacraments are so supernaturally endowed that even the human frailty of a priest administering this divine service cannot disavow or despoil their effectiveness. In fact, the Church has a term, *ex opere operato,* which is to say that the sacraments do not depend for their function upon the character of the priest, but that they confer grace and blessing by reasons of themselves, and by virtue of their work.

There are seven sacraments and, had you been born a Catholic, you would look upon them as divine mileposts along the true Christian path. The sacraments are: *Baptism, Confirmation, Penance, Holy Eucharist, Holy Orders, Holy Matrimony,* and *Extreme Unction.* You recognize that your life is inter-related "sacramentally" from birth to death, and that in each sacrament there is matter and form as well as grace and benefit.

BAPTISM

Baptism is administered by the priest as soon as possible after the birth of a child. It is a symbol of adoption and, more than a symbol, it is the very act of adoption of the child by God, making him an heir to God's riches and blessings.

Another significant aspect of this sacrament, in which the infant is lightly sprinkled with water, is the conviction that baptism is a necessary means of salvation. It is so important that should no priest be available, another baptized person may perform the act. Your Church believes that children who die unbaptized are deprived of seeing God in heaven. This does not mean that they are "lost" or that they are condemned to hell, but they do not receive the great glory and blessing of the "Beatific Vision." The authority is clear. Jesus said, "Unless a man is born again of water

and the Holy Spirit he cannot enter into the Kingdom of God."
(John 2:5). Your Church teaches that the "baptism of intention"
can save a soul, by which is meant that a dying person's sincere
and heartfelt longing for baptism may suffice when there is no one
around to perform the actual ceremony. The Church also believes
that adults who die without baptism or a knowledge of Christ can
be saved by the merits of Christ if they truly repent for their sins
before death.

CONFIRMATION

Confirmation played an important role in your life and left such
an impression that it can rarely, if ever, be erased. This sacrament
is the extension of baptism by the laying on of hands, an initiatory
rite by which, at the age of twelve or thirteen, you entered through
faith and intellectual understanding into the holiness of the
Church. To you it seems that your Church has wisely devised a
plan for the individual's spiritual development. It is sequential in
form: from infancy until you are about six years old, your parents
guide you in your religious beliefs; from six or seven until twelve
or thirteen, your teachers train you in the way you should go; at
confirmation, the priest brings you to the threshold of personal
responsibility.

The ceremony of confirmation is so sacred and impressive that,
as you kneel with the other confirmants in front of the altar, you
are convinced that God's will is being fulfilled in your life. As
the early apostles imparted the Holy Spirit by the laying on of
hands, so the bishop of your Church imparts the Holy Spirit to
you by a similar anointing. First he touches your head with chrism,
a mixture of olive oil and balsam, and then he lays his hands upon
you, saying, "I sign thee with the sign of the cross, and confirm
thee with the chrism of salvation, in the name of the Father, and
of the Son, and of the Holy Ghost." Confirmation is your Pentecostal experience, by which is meant that as the early Christians
received the baptism of the Holy Spirit on the day of Pentecost,
so you now receive it at the hands of the bishop.

PENANCE

The steps in the sacrament of Penance are: *confession, contrition, penance,* and *absolution.* This sacrament was impressed upon you at an early age. When you were six or seven you were instructed that Christianity meant living the good life; the kind of life Jesus would want you to live. Sin, to which all human beings are subject, was explained to you as *any act, word, or thought contrary to right reason and the law of God.* The Ten Commandments were a criteria by which your conduct could be measured. You were also told about an inner monitor, conscience, which warned you when you did wrong and endorsed your actions when you did right. You were taught the value of obedience to God's law, the extent of God's love, and the boundlessness of God's grace.

You were advised of the Church's method for helping you live the good life through the sacrament of Penance, and informed that whenever you fell into sin, God would be able and willing to forgive you and to cleanse you of sin, and to start you forward again on the right path if you were willing to do your part.

The sacrament of Penance was graphically demonstrated to you when, as a child, you made your first confession. You stepped into a confessional booth, found in every Catholic church, closed the door and knelt in front of a small grill above which hung a crucifix. You made the sign of the cross, remained silent for a moment and then said aloud, "Forgive me, Father, for I have sinned."

On the opposite side of the grill, in his own cubicle, the priest, unseen by you—as you by him—sat with his stole around his shoulders, ready to hear your confession. You did not give him your name, nor did he ask for it. You did not feel that you were confessing your sins to a man. Because going to confession was a part of your early religious training, it became your conviction that the confessional booth is a mystical corner in which the confrontation with Christ is no longer a mystery but becomes instead a reality.

The need for confessing your sins is impressed upon you every time you transgress one of the holy commandments. These Ten Commandments are an important guideline for your Christian life. You confess the grave sins of commission, remembering those thoughts and deeds which were done with the full consent of your will. You recognize the gravity of your sinning, but you remember that God sent Jesus into the world to save sinners by pardoning their sins.

The Church makes a distinction between two kinds of sins: mortal and venial. The first include those which cause the offender to forfeit the blessing of God's grace; namely, a deliberate sin of murder, the inflicting of great injury, or the sin of adultery. The second, venial sins, are violations of God's laws which do not alienate the sinner from God, but which, nonetheless, require penance; such sins as petty thievery, outburst of temper, lying, character defamation, and the like. The first, being the more severe, demand the fulfillment of certain requirements which will restore the sinner to a state of grace.

Having confessed your sins to God through the priest, you now hear the inspiring words in which he pronounces the absolution: "I absolve thee from thy sins in the name of the Father and of the Son and of the Holy Ghost." Through this pronouncement he has done his part as God's representative on earth, but it still remains for you to do your part before your sins are truly forgiven. You must be sure of two things: 1) contrition, which means heartfelt sorrow for sins committed and the determination to abstain from them in days to come; 2) satisfaction, by which is meant restitution. To replace what you have stolen, to ask forgiveness from those you have injured, to pray for those you have secretly offended—these are virtuous acts connected with satisfaction.

Since the Church believes there is a temporal as well as an eternal punishment connected with sin, it also believes it has the divine power to prescribe certain acts whereby the temporal punishment can be removed. These acts are of many kinds and are granted only where contrition is sincere. They include such recommendations as prayer, fasting, novenas, almsgiving, pilgrimages, and many other penitential practices.

THE HOLY EUCHARIST

The sacrament of Penance prepares you spiritually for the sacrament of Holy Eucharist, which is why you go to confession before partaking of Communion. Your first Communion, taken when you were six or seven after necessary counsel and instruction, was a thrilling and soul-lifting experience, an experience which, if your heart and soul are truly grateful, can be repeated every time you partake of this most significant of all the Church's rites. You prepare yourself for the Holy Eucharist by eating and drinking nothing for at least two hours before partaking of this sacrament. Perhaps you are one of those who comply with a former requirement of fasting from midnight until the sacrament is taken, for many of the faithful still adhere to this custom.

To participate in this sacred and mystical sacrament, you walk with folded hands to the communion rail which is near the altar. There you kneel to receive from the priest a sanctified wafer which his own hands place upon your tongue. Only it is not a wafer, so far as you are concerned. It is, in substance, the actual body of Christ.

This act of transubstantiation is a mystery which even Catholics themselves do not understand and which many non-Catholics openly deny and refuse to accept. Others call it superstition and magic and even "cannibalism," but this is because they do not comprehend the miracle of faith which places the communicant in a state of grace. You are convinced that Jesus himself instituted this Holy Eucharist when, at the last Supper, He took the bread and said, "This is My Body," and, taking the cup of wine, declared, "This is My Blood."

You accept these words literally, confident that when the wafer and the wine have been consecrated by the priest, "transubstantiation" takes place, which means that "His Body" has been actually converted into the "bread." Had you been born a Catholic, you would not only accept this as a fact, you would approach Communion with humble reverence, realizing that it is here that the spiritual union of your soul and Christ becomes a living reality.

The wine is not offered to you. The consuming of it is an act reserved for the priest. In the partaking of the consecrated bread, however, you have shared in the blood as well as in the flesh of Christ. This you truly believe and, as the sacrament of Penance cleanses your soul, so the Holy Eucharist leaves you feeling restored in body, mind, and spirit.

HOLY ORDERS

The sacrament of Holy Orders refers to the ordination of priests, extends through the entire structure of the Church, and is another distinctive sacrament in your faith. By means of it, the priest is endowed with a specific vocation; namely, the right to be Christ's representative in the work of redemption. At the Last Supper, when Jesus Christ, as the High Priest, instituted the Holy Eucharist, He also conferred upon the apostles the power to offer this sacrifice in His name. This bestowal, your Church teaches, was later followed by a ceremonial act in which the apostles took vows, declaring in the sight of God that they would live the religious life in a special way, and received a blessing by the laying on of hands.

You grew up with the utmost respect for your spiritual teachers, both priests and nuns, because you were convinced of their sincerity and their reverence for their holy calling. Rarely is there a Catholic boy who, at some period in his life, does not thoughtfully consider the priesthood as his vocation. Many Catholic girls somewhere along the way of life seriously contemplate entering convents to become teachers or nurses or members of one of the many orders of religious nuns. So great is the power of these people who have dedicated their lives to Christ and His Church that you often feel that they are the very life-blood of Catholicism.

In your youth your spiritual life took nourishment and direction from these holy priests and teachers. Sometimes you served as an altar boy and were privileged to assist the priest at Holy Mass. You learned a great deal about this service, for the Mass is the immortal setting that holds the precious gem of the Holy Eucharist. The Mass is the re-enactment of Christ's sacrifice in which He is continually lifted up for the sins of men and by means of which he is constantly glorified before His Father in heaven. The ceaseless vigilance and vitality of Roman Catholicism can be seen in the many observances of the Mass to which the Church is dedicated. The services are so arranged that everyone, no matter what his work or his station in life may be, can find an observance of the Mass in which he can participate. And whenever this happens, the priest is the intermediary between God and man. He is your spiritual parent and you reverently call him "Father."

Long years of training have gone into his preparation. Sacred vows have set him apart from other men. He dresses differently because of his position in the world. He does not marry because he has taken the vow of chastity so that his entire loyalty—body, mind, and spirit—may be dedicated to his calling. He observes special disciplines, reads special offices, and obeys the command of the Church set forth by the bishops, archbishops, cardinals, and the pope himself. He is a man under Holy Orders, your spiritual advisor, director, and friend.

HOLY MATRIMONY

It may seem paradoxical and even contradictory to non-Catholics, but to you it is clear that a celibate clergy can best advise you on the blessings and pitfalls of marriage. Matrimony is a sacrament, deeply spiritual in nature; and why, then, should not a man of God be best informed about its meaning?

You are convinced that idealistically no other religion puts the high credential upon married life or is so earnest about the sacredness of conjugal love as is Catholicism. Marriage is such a solemn undertaking that in the ceremony you and your marriage partner are actually administering this sacrament yourselves. The priest is merely the Church's witness, as other witnesses represent the families concerned.

The true Catholic could never enter marriage lightly or sensually, for he knows that the partner he takes is bound to him in an indissoluble union until death. It is like the marriage of Christ and His Church; sacred, inviolable, eternal. Divorce is absolutely forbidden in Roman Catholicism excepting in extremely rare cases involving adultery, insanity, or continual drunkenness.

Even then the Church requests that no other marriage take place until the death of the mate has dissolved the first marriage.

Marriage, you have been taught, has as its major function the propagation of the family of God. Because this is a sacred act, your Church opposes artificial methods of birth control in the belief that it leads to unnatural vice. The limitation of a family or a form of so-called "planned parenthood" is in accordance with Catholic doctrine only if the method is controlled by abstinence or the observance of the law of nature as evidenced in the so-called rhythm cycle.

Idealistically the Catholic home is a symbol of what the true Christian family should be like. It is built upon the foundation of faith and patterned after the glorification of God. Toward this end, *every home should be a shrine, every festive table an altar, every participant a worshiper.* Your home, like your Church, has many holy symbols: statues, candles, rosaries, sacred pictures, a Holy Bible, prayer books, and missals. In accordance with tradition, your family would recite certain prayers, fast on special days, attend church regularly, abstain from forbidden acts, and consult the priest on serious or perplexing matters.

Because of the sanctity of marriage and childbirth, the Catholic mother, after having brought a child into the world, often goes to the Church and gives thanks to God. Here she may also receive the special blessing of the priest who, sprinkling her with holy water, recites the 23rd Psalm and speaks a special prayer. This ceremony is called the "churching of women," and is said to have its roots in the Jewish rite of purification.

Because Holy Matrimony is the sacrament upon which the perpetuation of the Church in the world actually depends, it is understandable that Roman Catholicism should frown upon "mixed marriages." It is believed that it is far better for a Catholic to marry a Catholic and a non-Catholic to marry a non-Catholic than it is to cross denominational lines. The Church, which has systematically studied the course of mixed marriages, has decreed that varying religious beliefs in the home cause discord, resentment, and spiritual apathy. Often both parties are in danger of losing their faith.

Canon law, a law enacted by a church council and confirmed by the pope, forbids a Catholic or Catholics to be married by a non-Catholic minister. It also opposes mixed marriages being performed by a priest in the church, although a priest may solemnize such a ceremony in the sacristy or in the priest's home. Even then, the blessing of the ring or rings must be omitted and no nuptial Mass may be held. It is also necessary for both parties to sign the "marriage promises" in which it is agreed that children born of this union will be brought up in the Roman Catholic faith.

EXTREME UNCTION

As your life began with the sacrament of Baptism, so it is concluded with the sacrament of Extreme Unction. Meditating on this fact, you often feel that your religion is as compact as a holy book and that each chapter heading is sacramental. Life is, indeed, a story lived in Christ. Thus when the final pages are to be written, you look forward in faith to the continuation of life beyond this life.

The final sacrament of Extreme Unction is, actually, a seal of salvation. But it is not only a preparation for death; it may also be a means of healing so that life in this world may be extended. It consists of anointing the seriously ill with olive oil blessed by a bishop. As the priest touches the forehead of the afflicted with the oil, he says, "By this holy unction may the Lord pardon thee whatever faults thou hast committed."

Sometimes the priest anoints the eyes, ears, nose, mouth, hands, and feet, each time speaking a prayer. The comfort of this sacrament to the dying as well as to the loved ones who are bereaved is unspeakably great, for it brings the focus of faith upon the area of need. It consoles both the one who departs and those who remain. God, you sincerely believe, is pleased when His children do His will, and His will is best performed through the Holy Sacraments instituted by Christ, perpetuated by His Church, and performed by His chosen priests.

THE POWER AND GLORY OF THE CHURCH

Had you been born a Catholic, it would be difficult for you to express fully and completely the power and glory of your faith. It is too vast for words and too complex to be grasped in all its deepest meaning.

Its contrasts extend all the way from monks who live in monasteries secluded *from* the world to parish priests who live as comfortably as men *of* the world. It includes women who have entered cloisters to spend their entire lives in unseen meditation and prayer to parish women who are very much a part of teeming social life. It embraces miracles of healing like those which take place at Lourdes in France or Ste. Anne de Beaupré in Canada, but it does not deny the use of medical science and human healing skills. It approves of visions like those experienced by a Joan of Arc or a Saint Bernadette, but is extremely cautious of making claims for wholesale apparitions. It views with interest and understanding the stigmata of a St. Francis or a Theresa Neumann, but it allows hundreds of years to pass before it gives an estimate of their validity.

It believes in the outreach of science and accepts the efficacy of relics of the saints. It is supremely intellectual in its scholarship but almost childlike in its affection for the saints. It is a religion of joy and festivity, as seen in parish programs, while at the same time, it is a religion of sombre reflection, attested to by many austere devotional practices. Its liturgical calendar is so filled with holy days and sacred observances that there is hardly a period of the year in which the reminder of God's presence is not made known. It believes in the intercession of saints, in a personal devil, in purgatory, hell, heaven, the resurrection of the body, and a life to come.

It orders its adherents to be loyal to the Church and faithful to its teachings, to go to confession and communion at least once a year, and, whenever necessary, to sacrifice in the Church's behalf. It requires meatless days, particularly on Fridays, in remembrance of Christ's crucifixion. It stresses strict Lenten observances during the forty days preceding Easter. It believes in masses for the souls in purgatory, in the dogma of the Assumption (that the Blessed Virgin ascended bodily into heaven), allows the use of medals to honor God and the saints, and, in the recitation of the Lord's

Prayer, deletes the words, "For thine is the kingdom and the power and the glory, forever," because it is convinced that this was not a part of the original prayer as Jesus prayed it. It encourages its people to read the Bible, but advises them to use the Douay version which was translated from the Latin Vulgate, the Old Testament of which was published first in Douay, France, in 1610.

Your reverence for all these beliefs and practices synthesizes your religious and secular life into one spiritual unity. You are confident that the Church is ever with you and that you are ever with the Church. On special occasions, like the ordination of a priest who may be known to you, or at the consecration of a bishop or an archbishop of your diocese, you feel a great pride, for these are events in which you personally share.

THE DRAMA OF THE CHURCH

Within your lifetime you experienced the elevation of cardinals, those men who, appointed by the Holy Father, constitute the pope's council and are called the princes of the Church. The ceremony, held in St. Peter's in Rome, recalled the ancient rituals of your faith. At the appointed moment in this largest church in the world, a church designed by Michelangelo, the huge bronze doors swung open. Up the steps and through the doors marched towering Swiss guards wearing plumed hats, colorfully striped breeches and vests of yellow and red, looking as if they had emerged from a legend. Boots clopping sharply on the shining marble floors, heads up and their halberds flashing, they advanced down the roped-off aisles.

Behind them, against a pageantry of soldiers, archbishops, procurators, chaplains, monks, and priests, was the Holy Father borne on a throne carried on the shoulders of twelve stalwart men. "*Viva il Papa!*" cried the throng of worshiping spectators. As some threw kisses or wept for joy and fell to their knees in prayer, while many lifted up their rosaries and cheered, the spectacular procession moved by. The pope is a monarch, the emperor of Vatican State, as well as the Vicar of Christ over a spiritual kingdom that knows no bounds. As he sat in the gestatorial chair like a king, his court surrounded him; and in his holy train came the cardinals, resplendent in their scarlet robes and ermine capes. "Viva il Papa!" Though he is a king, he is one with his subjects—one in Christ. Making the sign of the cross over and over, he blessed the people as he was borne toward the high altar which rises over the tomb of St. Peter. Here, where the ninety-five lamps burn day and night, he stepped from his throne into the papal chair which stands immovable seven steps above the hallowed spot where the first pope, St. Peter, lies interred.

Against a background of pomp and ceremony, you heard the age-old chanted ritual and the sublime singing of the Sistine choir, out of the ceremonial Latin. You witnessed the elevation of the "princes of the faith" as one by one the incumbent cardinals brought the scarlet-clad candidates from the chapel. One by one they climbed the seven steps and kissed the Holy Father's ring, the "Fisherman's Ring," a symbol of the office of St. Peter. Then the Pontifical Master of Ceremonies dramatically raised the *galero,* the broad-brimmed red hat, over the head of each kneeling dignitary and intoned the blessing, "In praise of Almighty God and as an ornament of the Holy Apostolic See, receive now the red hat, distinctive of the Cardinal's dignity; it signifies that you must show yourself intrepid even unto shedding your blood for the exaltation of the Holy Faith, for the peace of the Christian people, and for the growth and glory of the Roman Church. In the name of the Father, and the Son, and the Holy Ghost."

THE FAITH OF THE CHURCH

These are your leaders, pledged to martyrdom, if need be, for the sake of the religion in which your life is rooted. And many in the past *have* given their lives. Many priests have been executed, as they were in the days of the Russian revolution, because they remained true to their vows and true to the Church. But neither death nor oppression has halted the growth of the faith. Nor even the passing of the Holy Father retards what you believe to be the steady forward march of the true Christian Church. In fact, during your lifetime you experienced the momentary shock and sadness of the death of Pope Pius XII, a much beloved prelate who was called the Pope of Peace. You mourned with the Church because of your love for him, and you rejoiced with your fellow Catholics when a new Sovereign was elected.

On that day, too, you felt yourself standing among the hundreds of thousands of faithful who crowded St. Peter's Square. You heard the bells toll out their ancient tones, broadcasting to the world that three days of secret balloting by the fifty-one cardinals of the Church had decreed God's will. For three days the multitudes had waited and watched, keeping eyes fixed on a slender chimney above the Vatican roof. In keeping with an old custom, a puff of white smoke would be the signal that the election had taken place. After each period of balloting the smoke had been black, however, but on October 17, 1958, it was suddenly white. The thrill that ran through the waiting crowd spread around the world as the news was flashed that Angelo Cardinal Roncalli had been chosen to fill the throne of St. Peter as the Bishop of Rome and the Vicar of Christ and had taken as his spiritual name Pope John XXIII in honor of the patron saint of his home parish in Venice.

A deafening cheer rose from St. Peter's Square as a fatherly figure appeared on the papal balcony. Dressed in the elaborate robes of his office, flanked by a group of church dignitaries, he raised his hands and spoke in a loud voice, *"Urbi et orbi!"*—"To the city and the world"; it was a benediction on the city and the world wherever the world extended. It blessed those behind the Iron Curtain and beyond the Bamboo Curtain; it went straight into the hearts of the Roman Catholic people—a half billion of them, with some 50,000,000 in the United States.

This is your Church and your faith which have come down to you through twenty ecumenical councils, the first of which was held in Nicea in 325 A.D. and the most recent of which was called by Pope John XXIII. This is your faith which has emerged out of apostolic times, is built upon great creeds, perpetuated by divine direction, and inspired by the Blessed Trinity: Father, Son, and Holy Ghost, each distinct, yet united and equal in essence.

Often, as the Holy Father himself has visualized, you, too, catch a glimpse of a world united, in which all people will live together as one family, each person distinct yet all united in the love and mercy of God, a people of whom it will be said that there is but one sheepfold and one Shepherd. "True peace," said Pope John XXIII in his first public utterance, "will not be given to citizens, to the peoples, to the nations if it is not first granted to their souls; because there can be no exterior peace if it is not the reflected image of interior peace."

Such would be your faith for yourself and your hope for the world, had you been born a Roman Catholic.

9

Had You Been Born
a Protestant

H AD YOU BEEN BORN A PROTESTANT, you would have discovered that although there are many Protestant groups,
there is one quality they all hold in common. They all believe that
man's quest for God is a matter of love and will, and that it must
be free. Protestantism, you would have realized, is much like
democracy. As there are fifty states in the union, all different, but
comprising America, so there are nearly two hundred distinctive
denominations comprising Protestantism.

THE "DEMOCRACY" OF PROTESTANTISM

Just as people in certain states believe their states are best, so
some Protestant worshipers believe their denominations are best.
You would never persuade certain New Englanders to live in the
Midwest, nor could you lure certain Midwesterners to New Eng-
land. To live where they wish to live is the American privilege.
You would never persuade some liberal Protestants ever to become
fundamentalists, or some fundamentalists ever to become liberals.
To believe what they wish to believe is the Protestant privilege.

Protestantism has many privileges and that is why a great

167

responsibility rests upon its followers, just as a democracy puts a responsibility upon its adherents. For example, Protestantism knows no authority other than that of the Scriptures, and this authority is often interpreted in various ways. *Protestantism knows no law other than divine love, and no truer spiritual credential than the awareness of serving God in thought, word, and deed.* These things are often interpreted differently by different groups, but every Protestant believes that the indwelling Christ is the door of perception to all that God is and all that He has devised for mankind in this life and in the life to come. Such convictions would be part of the heritage passed on to you, had you been born a Protestant.

Somewhere along the way you would also have your doubts and misgivings about Protestantism. The word itself would bother you. You would ask yourself, "What are we Protestants protesting?" A bit of research, however, would tell you that the word "Protestant" was first used in 1529. At the Diet of Spires in Germany, Charles V declared that expansion of the new evangelical religion should be suppressed. Democratic Christians protested. They issued their own ultimatum. They said, "In matters concerning God's honor and the salvation of souls, each man must for himself stand before God and give account!" From this declaration Protestantism took its name and to this day those who sincerely subscribe to the spirit of this statement are participants in the Protestant tradition.

Despite such historical justification, Protestantism is, for most Protestants, a misnomer, but no one has ever come up with a better word to describe those Christians who are not of the Roman Catholic or Eastern Catholic persuasion.

THE ROOTS OF PROTESTANTISM

Historically, the organized Protestant groups go back to the Reformation, which was spearheaded by Martin Luther in 1517, but there were other important reform movements before the time of Luther. Groups like the Moravian Brethren, the Waldenses, and the Anabaptists were of the opinion that Catholicism as expressed in the early creeds and councils had digressed far from the apostolic church. Individuals of deep commitment like John Huss, John Wycliffe, William Occam, Girolamo Savonarola, Gerhard Groot, and others were convinced that God had given them revelations, too, and that they were called upon to correct what they believed to be corrupt conditions.

This is what Luther felt called to do. Educated and disciplined as a priest in the Augustinian order, he was led to rediscover the New Testament doctrine of salvation which persuaded him that "man is justified by faith and not by works," that there is a "priesthood of all believers," that the Bible is the only infallible rule for "faith and conduct," and that the "Holy Spirit alone can aid in the true interpretation of the Word of God."

These four fundamental principles, Protestants believe, are rooted in the Apostolic Church, the Church inspired by Christ which developed in the days of the apostles. Protestants are convinced that they belong in the spiritual succession of the universal church. Luther, contending that Catholicism had deserted these basic principles, challenged Rome to debate and clarify 95 inconsistencies and inaccuracies which he enumerated and boldly posted on the door of his church in Wittenberg, Germany.

These "95 theses" became the groundwork for a mighty religion which was to take the name "Lutheranism" and which rapidly became a popular Christian movement. It spread through Germany and Scandinavian countries at a time when Europe was on the threshold of an intellectual, artistic, and spiritual renaissance. It was a new religious planet, or the old apostolic light returned. In its orbit were other movements and other leaders: John Calvin and John Knox, who instituted Presbyterianism; Huldreich Zwingli, who influenced the rise of Reformed groups; Thomas Munzer, who sparked a form of mysticism among the Anabaptists; and Menno Simons, who gave rise to the Mennonites.

There were groups like the Baptists, who felt that they, too, had always perpetuated the church of the early apostles. And, later, there were movements like Methodism, the Disciples of Christ, Churches of Christ, United Brethren, Congregationalism, and many more which arose as a re-emphasis of the life and beliefs of the "apostolic tradition."

PROTESTANT BAPTISM

The differences among these various groups would be revealed to you in many ways. For example, at an early age you would very likely have been baptized in your particular parental faith. You would learn that some Protestant groups baptize infants, others baptize only adults. Some use the mode of sprinkling—the minister dipping his fingers into water and moistening the candidate's head and imparting a blessing. Some churches prescribe that the minister "pour" the water out of his cupped hands. Others employ immersion, insisting this was the practice in the early church. Some immerse once, others three times. Some immerse face forward into the water, others backward.

Certain Protestant faiths consider baptism a mystical rite, a means of grace, forgiveness, purification, regeneration. In other groups, baptism is a christening ceremony during which the child is named. But whenever and wherever Protestants are baptized, it is believed that baptism unites the believer with Christ. It is an act of holiness, and in this respect it adheres to the best in Protestant tradition which insists that, despite all ceremonialism, religion must first be an affair of the heart. Idealistically, religion is a matter of personal commitment and freedom of will.

CONFIRMATION

Had you been born a Protestant, you would never be stampeded into holiness. You would take the baptismal vows upon yourself only when you had reached an age of accountability. Then you would become a catechumen, ready for instruction in the Bible and the catechism of your particular denomination. Here, too, the great latitude among the many Protestant groups defies generalization. Some denominations require a prescribed course of study prepared by their headquarters, some use historic catechisms, some introduce modern interpretations of the Bible, others emphasize dogma, church history, meditative techniques; but the basis of study is always designed to allow freedom in the search for truth.

Your first step on the highway of faith would be taken on the day of your confirmation, and you would learn that Protestantism is never, in any sense, a dead-end street. Confirmation, like baptism, varies as much as the denominations themselves vary, but in almost all groups confirmation means that you have reached spiritual responsibility. You are now admitted into church membership, with all its privileges and responsibilities, and you become a member of the congregational family which is the heart of Protestant life.

Confirmation is a constant reminder that it is up to you what you will do with your Christian profession, the essence of which is poignantly phrased, "The kingdom of God is within you." This is the dynamic behind the "priesthood of believers" and the power inherent within the infallible Book. Protestantism continually assures you that it has always specialized in the individual's right to discover this kingdom of God in his own way.

Because of this you find nothing incongruous about the many divisions in Protestantism. Its democratic nature, which allows the seeker freedom of the quest, gradually impresses you with a kind of sacred idealism. You realize that it is as right for others to be loyal to their faith as it is for you to be true to yours. To admit diversity in religion is not to say that there is more than one absolute faith, but it does imply that there can be various expressions of the one.

UNITY IN DIVERSITY

But you would often wonder just where Protestantism begins and where it ends. Going into an Episcopalian church, you would find it quite "Catholic" in its "setting" and its service. You would discover that most Anglicans object to being classified as Protestants. They would remind you that the Church of England had broken with Rome before Protestant doctrines were ever accepted by the English people and that Anglicanism represents the unbroken line of apostolic tradition. You would be told by some Anglicans that their religion is half way between evangelical Protestantism and Roman Catholicism and that it embodies the most essential elements in each.

Anglicanism was, originally, a national church. Lutheran,

Reformed, and Presbyterian churches were international. Lutheranism was and still is more formalistic and more liturgical than most Protestant bodies and some Lutherans, too, would resist the term "Protestant" as an identification of their Christian status.

You would discover that some Protestant denominations (like the Methodist Church) are Arminian; that is, they believe in free will. Others are Calvinistic (like the Presbyterians and the Dutch Reformed) believing in a form of predestination or limited atonement. Still others, notably the Pentecostals, believe in a mystical experience, the baptism of the Holy Spirit, and are quite emotional about their religion. Some Protestants (as for example, certain Adventists) insist on observing the seventh day as the Sabbath. Several (like certain Holiness groups) do not allow instrumental music, and there are those which, like certain Quaker groups, insist on complete quietude. Some Protestants are Unitarians, some Trinitarians; some are humanists, deists, theists, pantheists, spiritualists, dualists, monists; some are orthodox, neo-orthodox and some quite heterodox! There are even Protestant agnostics and Protestant monks. Heterogeneous, complex, and amazing is the globe-circling spiritual community called by the paradoxical term: *Protestantism.*

If you were to ask a member of the Church of Jesus Christ of Latter Day Saints whether Mormons are Protestants, his answer would very likely be, "Mormonism is neither Protestant nor Catholic nor anything else excepting Christianity *plus.*" He would mean plus the teachings of Joseph Smith and the revelations of the Book of Mormon and doctrines not commonly found in Protestantism. Yet, in the public mind, Mormons are commonly classified as Protestants. So, too, are the members of the Reorganized Church of Latter Day Saints; the members of the Pentecostal groups, Jehovah's Witnesses, Christian Scientists, members of the Unity School of Christianity, the healing and preaching evangelists, the non-Catholic radio ministers and, in short, every Christian who is not a Roman Catholic or an Eastern Catholic or an Anglo-Catholic is looked upon by the "public" as a Protestant.

If you went among the snake handlers in Tennessee and asked one of their preachers what denomination he belonged to, he would very likely exclaim, "Praise the Lord, I'm a Protestant holiness man!"

Again and again you would encounter Protestant groups whose way of life is unique, distinctive, and, occasionally, tremendously austere. Such people are found among the Mennonites and the Amish and other followers of what is historically called the Anabaptist tradition. They urge their members to live the simple life, to assert their belief in pacifism, to accept the literal interpretation of the Bible, and insofar as is humanly possible to be "in the world and not of it."

Certain Mennonite, Amish, and Hutterite people often wear distinctive attire, such as hook-and-eye jackets, broad-brimmed "preachers'" hats for the men and prayer caps for the women. Married men let their beards grow. Young people are ordered not to go to colleges or universities for fear secular education might lure them away from God. Some groups use horses and buggies instead of automobiles. Amish people refuse to take oaths, refuse to vote, refuse to become embroiled in the affairs of the community or the world. These, too, are part of Protestantism's fabulous family which under a variety of denominational labels encircles the world.

GLOBAL PROTESTANTISM

Wherever Protestantism goes it establishes religious beachheads by starting missions, schools, and hospitals; and by developing a program of lay activities through the solemn dedication of the Christian life. Today there are approximately 300,000,000 Protestants in the world out of a total Christian population of about 1,000,000,000. Of the nearly 120,000,000 members of Christian churches in the United States, 80,000,000 are Protestants.

The essential unity in Protestantism is centralized in a major organization known as the National Council of Churches of Christ in the U.S.A. Here the growing evidence of ecumenicity is graphically portrayed. The Council is a spiritual union of some thirty constituent bodies representing nearly 50,000,000 persons. It is closely related to the World Council of Churches whose headquarters is in Geneva, Switzerland. Generally speaking, it advocates a liberal Protestant expression, which means that it allows for great latitude of thought on such important matters as the person and mission of Christ, Biblical scholarship, and faith and morals.

Its fundamentalist counterpart is the well-established American Council of Christian Churches which is opposed to modernism and the liberal trend. Other great national and international organizations are the World Methodist Council, the World Conference of International Pentecostal Churches, Lutheran World Federation, and many more; while Protestant missionary activity runs the gamut from home missionaries on Indian reservations in America to the impressive work of the lonely figure, Dr. Albert Schweitzer, laboring in the heart of Africa. The vastness of this picture would unfold for you as you took your place in one of the 400,000 churches which Protestants have built around the world.

THE BONDS OF MATRIMONY

If and when you contemplated marriage, your wedding would very likely be solemnized by a Protestant minister—eighty percent of Protestant weddings are. Others are "civil ceremonies" performed by a judge, justice of the peace, or, in some states, by other city officials.

Perhaps yours would be a church wedding, for marriages in Protestant sanctuaries are impressive ceremonies. They are performed "in the sight of God and His holy angels," and the bride and groom pledge their troth, "for better or worse, for richer for poorer, in sickness or in health, till death us do part." Frequently marriages are performed in a small chapel connected with the church, in the pastor's study or in the parsonage or manse.

Christian love, the ceremony makes clear, should be the dominant factor in family life. In the Protestant perspective on marriage, the love of Christ should rule the heart and direct the mind. "The bonds of matrimony," says a Protestant Book of Worship, "is an honorable estate, instituted of God in the time of man's innocency, confirmed by the teaching of our blessed Saviour, and compared by Saint Paul to the mystical union which subsists between Christ and His Church."

A Protestant service may be as elaborate or as simple as the marrying parties wish, but all Protestant weddings consistently close with a spiritual benediction upon the solemnization of the vow. Some ministers pronounce a blessing which says, ". . . so live together in this life, that in the world to come ye may have everlasting life."

PROTESTANTISM IS A RELIGION OF THE LAITY

Your devotion to your church would deepen when your own children were baptized and when you started taking them to Sunday School and the church's services. Protestantism has nearly 300,000 Sunday Schools serving 40,000,000 Sunday School members in the United States. You would also enroll your children in vacation Bible Schools and summer camps, in young people's fellowships and spiritual brigades, for which Protestantism is famous. Protestantism is becoming more and more a religion in which the laity plays an important role. Laymen's organizations, women's associations, and youth movements represent a new dynamism in the work of the church. *Religion, the Protestant believes, must be activated by the people in the parish and demonstrated at the congregational level.* This is done by the laity who comprise the church boards, who teach in the Sunday Schools, conduct Daily Vacation Bible Schools, carry on missionary programs, and engage in countless activities that integrate religion and the church into community life.

Had you been born a Protestant, you would probably observe prayer before meals, and religion would often be a subject of discussion and debate in the family circle. You would subscribe to at least one religious publication. You would own at least two Bibles. You would buy and read at least three religious books a year.

True to statistics and true to yourself, the older you became, the more you would love and support your church. This is not to say you would attend every worship service or contribute as much as you should to the church's program. Only some 40% of the

Protestants who belong to a church attend the services regularly. Total financial contribution per member is in the neighborhood of $50 per year, but Protestant tithing and Protestant church attendance are on the increase, and love for the church is a vital, abiding reality in Protestant life.

HOLY COMMUNION

This reality, as far as a Protestant's relation to his church is concerned, is best expressed in the sacraments. While Roman Catholicism has seven sacraments—baptism, the Eucharist, confirmation, marriage, ordination, penance, and extreme unction—Protestantism generally observes two: baptism and the Lord's Supper. Had you been born a Protestant, you would find a mystical meaning in both of these sacred observances. Baptism, enjoined in the Great Commission (Matthew 28:19,20), symbolizes the union of the believer with Christ. Communion is symbolical of the redemption affected by Christ's death.

Some denominations, like the Disciples of Christ, observe communion each Sunday. Others administer it at stated times during the year. It generally consists of a ritual in which the member partakes of a bit of bread and drinks a sip of wine (usually unfermented grape juice) in memory of Christ's suffering and death. Whether your church invites you to come forward to the communion rail or whether you receive the bread and wine in the pew, whether your church believes that the elements are the Real Presence or merely symbolical, the Lord's Supper is so intimately associated with the heart of faith that every communion service represents a holy pilgrimage for the true worshiper.

Often during times of sickness, holy communion is administered as a special act of worship and faith. And frequently, when death is impending, the sacrament is requested by faithful Protestants.

LIFE AFTER DEATH

What does Protestantism believe about life after death? Here, again, you would find great diversity of interpretation yet surprising unity of belief. Generally speaking, Protestantism agrees that the soul of man is eternal. It believes that those who love God, who are "saved" through the redemptive work of Christ, will live forever in fellowship with God. Personal immortality is almost universally accepted by Protestantism. It finds its proof not in pure reason or pragmatic arguments, but in God's Word. It believes in the resurrection of Christ and in His promise that those who "die in Him" shall inherit life beyond the grave.

Protestantism trusts in the goodness of God and believes that since God is good, He will not annihilate what He has made in His own image. This argument, based on the ethical in God's plan and the ethical in human life, is one of Protestantism's most impressive justifications for life after death. *Belief in Jesus, who perfectly portrayed God's love, and belief in immortality are so closely bound together that one without the other is incomplete in Protestant thought.*

Heaven and hell are actual "places" according to some Protestants, and actual "conditions" according to others. Some believe there is a "second chance" in the life to come, others do not. Some believe in an intermediary realm between heaven and hell. Some teach a "resurrection of the body"; others reject such a literal interpretation. Some groups strongly oppose cremation; others permit it. But all agree that on the matter of life after death, no greater and more explicit word was ever spoken than that of Jesus when He said, "I am the resurrection and the life . . . he that believeth in Me, though he were dead, yet shall be live; and whosoever liveth and believeth in Me, shall never die." (John 11:25).

All Protestant groups agree that man is possessed of a soul or, better stated, man is a soul which, for this earthly life, has been given a physical body. For an allotted time the body is the temple of the soul (or spirit) and it is the duty of the individual to care for both body and soul as a Christian obligation. The Protestant ideal, the ultimate ideal as far as spiritual attainment is concerned, is found in the injunction, "Be ye therefore perfect, even as your Father which is in heaven is perfect." (Matthew 5:48).

THE PROTESTANT WAY OF LIFE

Most Protestants believe perfection to be a conceivable but unattainable goal. The challenge to perfection has added the Christian virtues of faith, hope, and love to the four older cardinal virtues of wisdom, courage, temperance, and justice. Schleiermacher, a Protestant theologian, maintained that true religion consists of recognizing all of our duties as divine commandments. German Pietists of the 17th and 18th centuries stressed the belief that faith is "dead" unless it is demonstrated in upright living. Protestantism is more a way of life than an intellectual attitude. The Protestant may not always live the good life. He may, as has been said, despair of attaining perfection, but the ideal is ever before him and spurs him on to realize his highest self.

If the Protestant's assignment is to be "perfect" even as "God is perfect," his social obligation is no less idealistic. He is urged to love his neighbor as himself. To gain his life he must lose it. To be greatest he must be least of all. To reign, he must serve. To receive, he must be willing to give. To demonstrate the highest love, he is challenged to lay down his life for his friends.

A PERSONALIZED FAITH

Had you been born a Protestant, the term "social gospel" would be more than a phrase. It would represent an active force for social betterment in the form of schools, hospitals, orphanages, homes for the aged, urban and rural improvement and, most of all, active participation in contributing to the over-all concept of the "Kingdom of God." Protestantism's social consciousness is so real and vital that its pursuit has often created unity among divergent Protestant groups. Liberals, conservatives, fundamentalists, agnostics, deists, and theists, new groups as well as old within the framework of Protestantism share a common concern for the improvement of mankind around the world. They are, or seek to be, Good Samaritans, who accept responsibility for the conditions of human life as well as for the improvement of those conditions.

Peace of mind, peace of soul, positive thinking, healthful living, the will to believe are all a part of Protestantism's contemporary storehouse of faith. "Ask and you shall receive," "Seek and ye shall find," "Greater things than these shall you do," "Bring your tithes into the storehouse and prove me now, saith the Lord, if I will not open the windows of heaven for you,"—these and many more are Protestantism's words to live by. In an age full of frustrations, tensions, anxiety, and insecurity, a wave of "do-the-possible-and-God-will-do-the-impossible" has become a Protestant conviction. From the most ardent fundamentalists to the ultraliberals, some form of "power through God-power" has been introduced to meet a people's need.

Had you been born a Protestant, you would be urged to use your faith for the solution of *your* needs. You would find Protestant healing services, pastoral clinics, suggested affirmations, daily meditations, and all sorts of books and aids ready to help you. You would find ministers appealing to you as if you had the capacity within yourself—"the God-presence"—to meet any problem and to triumph over any impending defeat.

Because of the variegated pattern of Protestantism there are, of course, many shades of emphasis in this gospel of abundance. Theologians, though affected by it and even inclined to practice its techniques, argue against it because it lacks theological depth and intellectual content. They look with scholarly dissent upon the theological emptiness of modern personalized faith. But the practicers of these "spiritual techniques" look with equal dissent upon the theological and academic passion of their accusers.

PROTESTANTISM AND APPLIED CHRISTIANITY

The average Protestant affirms that neither creed nor theology can ever take primacy over the Scriptures. If Jesus and the disciples healed the sick, there is no reason not to look for healing miracles today. If the Master promised that those who follow Him should do works as great or greater than His own, why not expect great things from those who live the Christ-life in the modern world?

This is not to say that the theologian has no voice in Protestantism. He surely has, but his voice is rarely understood by the people in the pews. Few Protestant lay members could tell you anything about the theological or philosophical concepts of such men as Kierkegaard, Barth, the Niebuhrs, Brunner, Tillich, or Bultmann. The work of these men is far beyond the normal interest of the Protestant laity. Right or wrong, for better or worse, today's Protestant is primarily concerned with the application of the precepts and practices of Christ in the workaday life of the individual.

An interpreter for the people, such as a Harry Emerson Fosdick; a preacher to the people, such as a Ralph Sockman; a mystic among the people, such as a Rufus Jones; a spiritual technician, such as a Norman Vincent Peale; a zealous evangelist such as a Billy Graham; and most of all, someone who demonstrates the Christian life in selfless service like a Frank Laubach in his exhaustless work among the world's illiterates or the selfless service of a Dr. Larimer Mellon in Haiti; these are the men who would influence you most, had you been born a Protestant.

The term "Protestantism" as a mark of Christian identification would not seem overly important to you. Unlike the Catholic, you would believe that even if your church should pass away, your faith will never pass away. Unlike the Jew, you are not intent on perpetuating a tradition, excepting the tradition of democratic Christian thought. Unlike the Moslem, you have no prescribed acts of worship, unless it is the act of faith. *Unlike the followers of other great religions, you believe in the daring—some say dangerous—practice of exercising private judgment in interpreting the Bible, believing that the Holy Spirit will aid you in your interpretation if your search is sincere.*

Had you been born a Protestant, you would feel sure that your religion is rich in hope and peace. You would believe that its God is a God of joy. Aware of your sins, you would seek God for forgiveness; grateful for the promise of salvation, you would praise Him for His grace.

PROTESTANT UNITY IS A REALITY

You would join with Protestants throughout the world in a universal creed, "I believe in God, the Father Almighty. . . ."

You would unite with Christians everywhere in praying, "Our Father, which art in heaven. . . ." You would be sensitive to the beliefs of all men because of your conviction that "As many as are led by the Spirit of God, they are the sons of God." You would observe the great holy seasons and holy days of the liturgical year: Advent, Christmas, Epiphany, Lent, Good Friday, Easter, Pentecost. You would express your faith in such observances as World Day of Prayer, Laymen's Sunday, Mission Festivals, Harvest Home observances, Mother's Day, and others.

Protestant hymns reflect your deepest faith in special ways. "A Mighty Fortress is our God," "The Church's One Foundation," "Joy to the World," "Up From the Grave He Arose," "There's a Wideness in God's Mercy," "This is My Father's World." Had you been born a Protestant, you would know and love these hymns. You would also be acquainted with gospel songs and Negro spirituals.

Wherever you went in the world you would hear Protestantism singing, in city churches and country chapels, in distant mission fields and in denominational schools, singing songs of faith which tell the gospel story. One song has been translated into more than sixty languages. It is Protestantism's marching song and, as you sang it, you would realize that most non-Protestants have a hard time believing it, for this song, "Onward Christian Soldiers," proclaims in splendidly spirited style, *We are not divided, all one body we! One in hope and doctrine, one in charity!"*

Protestantism's amazing diversity makes it difficult for these words to sound convincing. Yet, they express the Protestant ideal, not fully realized, not wholly demonstrated, but apparent and real in the heart of the true Protestant believer.

"Protestantism," said an old medical doctor, "ought to remind a man of spring. Or spring of Protestantism. It is new life beginning to move. New cells splitting up. It is like the process of mitosis— cell division, cell growth. The multiplication of cells is one of the manifestations of an inherent vital force. You say there are some two hundred Protestant denominations? There are more than two hundred chromosomes in primitive germ cells. I say that's good. It is not unification that makes life move. It's diversity. It is not somebody saying, 'I speak for 300,000,000 Christians!' It is rather every Protestant in the world testifying to what religion has done for him and letting us decide what it can do for us. That is what faith is, whether you like it or not. That is what I call unity in diversity. And that, my friend, is exactly why and how Protestantism came into the world."

To all of which you would no doubt say, "Amen!" had you been born a Protestant.

Conclusion
And So It Seems to Me

N OW THAT YOU HAVE PUT YOURSELF in the other person's
place, what have you learned?

Where do you go from here?

Perhaps you, too, will agree with me as I agreed with Vinoba
Bhave, the "walking saint of India" to whom I referred in the
chapter on Hinduism. I walked with him one morning at four
o'clock. Along with a group of his followers, I set out upon the
shadowy Indian road. As the sun spread its first warming light
over the countryside, I realized that my several hundred companions—farmers, businessmen, monks, and even mothers with
children—represented many cultures and creeds. As the light became brighter I saw that the man with whom I had been walking
silently through the dark was thin and emaciated, wearing a white
homespun *dhoti* and thick-lensed spectacles. He shuffled along so
rapidly in his worn sandals that I had difficulty keeping up. Suddenly he glanced my way. A smile lit up his bearded face and he
said in English, "I think if Jesus were on earth He would be
walking with us this morning." Then he added, "I am sure He is."

This was Vinoba Bhave graphically expressing a Gandhian
phrase: "If a man reaches the heart of his own religion, he has
reached the heart of others, too."

And it seemed to me that here I found one answer: *the spirit*

183

inherent in religions is found to be one spirit when we truly put ourselves in the other person's place.

I found another hint of what this spiritual interchange can mean when I met Dr. Albert Schweitzer in Africa. I will long remember how he stood on the improvised dock on the edge of the rusty Ogooue river. Dressed in white, wearing a white pith helmet, he extended both hands in greeting as I stepped from the dugout canoe. But I will remember even longer the Schweitzer spirit. It is a synthesis of many faiths.

Few of our contemporaries—in fact, few men in history—are so unidentifiable denominationally as is Dr. Schweitzer. Lutherans insist he belongs to them "parentally"; Unitarians are convinced he is in their camp theologically; Presbyterians claim him traditionally; Evangelicals, historically; and liberal Baptists, spiritually. To the Quakers, he is a symbol of pacifism; to the Congregationalists, a sign of healthy humanism; and, if he were a Catholic, to them he would be a saint, someone to be canonized. He believes in the Hindu concept of non-violence, but he has Christianized it; he is so close to the Jain teaching of *ahimsa* that he practices it. He sees similarities between Buddha and Luther, and he notes that passive resistance passed on from Jesus into the life of Gandhi.

As I walked with Schweitzer through the aisles of his jungle hospital, a hospital pitifully over-crowded with native patients who have found in this Alsatian a man of exceptional mercy, and as I accompanied him in a visit to the nearby leper village, it seemed to me that his reverence for life is undergirded by his reverence for man's everlasting quest for truth. He is unconcerned whether the quest be by the way of suffering or service, or whether the man is white or black or what his faith may be. Reverence, to Schweitzer, is not a creed, but an act; it is not a matter of profession, but a matter of deed.

His views on inter-religious relations were stated clearly when he said, *"Impart as much of your faith as you can to those who walk the road of life with you, and accept as something precious that which comes back to you from them."*

And then later, it seemed to me, I found something else, something that was impressed upon me by another man in another part of the world, but in a similar arc in the circle of faith. It was Dr. Daisetz T. Suzuki, the Zen scholar, who reminded me that as we enter into the beliefs of others, we may find some of our own beliefs personified.

One day in Dr. Suzuki's home in Atami, Japan, I told him about a pet theory of mine that we believe what we will to believe. First comes the wish, and then the will, then the rationale, and then our insistence that what we have found is truth. I cited as an example the dogma of the Assumption, which affirms that Mary the Mother of Jesus ascended bodily into heaven.

"Who saw her ascend?" I asked and answered my own question by saying, "No one. Yet people have the will to believe it. Who saw her?"

Suzuki was silent for a long moment. Then he said softly and with reverence, "I saw her."

It seemed to me just then, in the silence of the room, that the simple and gracious *hina dan,* the little altar so typical of Japanese homes, was neither Shinto nor Buddhist nor Confucianist nor Christian, but rather a symbol of universal faith. Quietly I found myself saying, "I saw her, too." And I knew that *feeling, no less than experience, can be a source of spiritual knowledge just as intuition can at times be stronger and stranger than the stubborn conclusions of the intellect.*

So this, too, was another answer.

It seemed to me then, as it had often in the past, that if you are a Protestant and you wish to understand and enter into the experience of the Roman Catholic, you can do it neither by standing outside the church nor by arguing against the church's claims. You must go inside.

And if you are a Catholic and you would understand Protestantism, you will never do it unless you stand where the Protestant stands. You cannot look over the wall of preconceived ideas and get an honest impression. You must, for a little while, enter into the spirit and the tradition of all the Protestant cherishes and believes.

This must be done by the interrelation of all sincere believers all around the great mandala of faith in which, all too long, each group has lived in its own restricted sphere, unaware of its close kinship with other groups. With hatred and suspicion increasing in the world, the warning has become all too real: we must learn to live together or none of us will live.

The great hope for a new order and a new era lies in the new spiritual exchange which is growing in the hearts of people in every living faith. A vision of the universality of religion is moving among free people everywhere because they have common concerns, common needs, and common causes. These problems themselves will bring about the realization that whenever we investigate the other person's way of life, we reinvestigate our own. And whoever approaches religion in this way is not going to condemn anything, but is going to discover that religion's likenesses are greater than its differences.

This new dimension in religion already exists, and a spiritual unity is seen beyond and above sectarian disunity. It includes the physicist whose thoughts have penetrated outer space, the historian whose study has followed the footprints of God through the rise and fall of civilizations, the scientist who has opened the secret doors of the inner mind, the philosopher who has revealed a harmony in the once inharmonious schools of thought, the educator who perceives a divine power beyond as well as within the intellectual process, the healer of bodies who knows that resources of health reside within the God-nature of every man, the industrialist and the laborer who have caught on to a workable ethic in their business dealings, the theologian who recognizes a divine power as the common ground of all beings—in short, men and women of every walk of life who look upon religion as a quest and an adventure in search and discovery.

The full circle of spiritual truth will be completed only when we realize that, but for a destiny not fully understood, we might actually *have* been born in the other person's faith.

About the Author

Marcus Bach has since youth been drawn to the knowledge of people as they worship; as a scholar and writer, his religious inquiry is characterized by sympathy with the believer in whom faith is embodied. He is presently a Professor in the School of Religion of the State University of Iowa, devoting much of his time to research and travel abroad in the interest of inter-religious and inter-cultural activity. A frequent companion is his wife Lorena, whose camera has recorded the memorable scenes and encounters of travels that have taken them throughout Asia and the Orient, meeting —on grounds of friendship—peoples of every faith.

Dr. Bach is the author of a dozen books, twenty plays, and numerous articles which have appeared in Coronet, Reader's Digest, Christian Herald, The American Weekly and many other magazines. Prentice-Hall will publish his book now in progress, a popular history of the world's religions.